Culture Clash
in Americca

FOUR PLAYS

Bordertown SAN DIEGO & TIJUANA

Nuyorican Stories NEW YORK CITY

Mission Magic Mystery Tour SAN FRANCISCO

Anthems WASHINGTON, D.C.

THEATRE COMMUNICATIONS GROUP
2003

Culture Clash in Americca is published by Theatre Communications Group, Inc.,
520 Eighth Ave., 24th Floor New York, NY 10018-4156.

This publication is made possible in part with funds from the New York State
Council on the Arts, a State Agency.

TCG books are exclusively distributed to the book trade by Consortium Book
Sales and Distribution, 1045 Westgate Dr., St. Paul, MN 55114

Library of Congress Cataloging-in-Publication Data

Culture clash in American / by Culture Clash.
p.cm.
ISBN 1-55936-216-2 (Paperback : alk. paper)
1. American drama–California–San Francisco. 2. San Diego (Calif.)–Drama.
3. Mexican American Border Region–Drama. 4. New York (N.Y.)–Drama.
5. Puerto Ricans–New York (State)–New York–Drama. 6. Mission District
(San Francisco, Calif.)–Drama. 7. San Francisco (Calif.)–Drama. I. Culture
Clash (comedy troupe)
PS572.S33 C85 2003
812'.6080979461–dc21
2003000819

Cover image by Matthias Clamer/Getty Images
Back cover photograph by Modern Multiples
Cover and text design by Lisa Govan
First printing, May 2003

Culture Clash
in Americca

Contents

Preface

By Guillermo Gómez-Peña

In the mid-1980s, the Chicano arts movement was undergoing a profound internal crises. Aesthetic stagnation, self-defensive nationalism, incendiary gender and generational conflicts were but a few symptoms. At the same time, the Chicano-Latino/a communities were becoming much more diversified, demanding brand-new artistic languages capable of articulating our new ethnic, gender and political complexities.

Then came Culture Clash, a collective of locos and locas who defied all existing categories. To begin with, the original troupe consisted of two Chicanos (Montoya and the late José Antonio Burciaga), two Central Americans (Salinas and Siguenza) and two lesbians (Marga Gómez and Monica Palacios), and all of them had more than one artistic interest. Though they chose to occupy the codified space of American "comedy," they were also play-wrights, spoken-word poets, visual artists, filmmakers and activists. Humor was their main strategy, true; but they were too serious, troubled and strange to be considered mere "comedians."

Montoya, Salinas and Siguenza opened a can of worms. In fact, perhaps their great contribution to Chicano-Latino culture was to dare to turn the gaze inward, become self-critical and put into question everything held sacred by our communities. In this process, they expanded the conceptual repertoire of permissible subject matter and dared to tackle extremely sensitive issues which up to that point were a mere internal conversation or gossip within "la comunidad." In addition to other taboo subject matters, they poked fun at gender and generational conflicts, our own *tapadismo,* the touchy Chicano-Cuban schism, and the problematic relationship between Chicanismo and mainstream culture. They turned the much-touted "Latino boom" upside down and made fun of our then still untouchable cultural heroes, both the real ones and the prefabricated ones. Thanks to their venom, we can say that Chicanismo loosened up and became much more fluid, and self-reflexive.

In the 1990s, Culture Clash engaged in a number of dangerous crossover adventures without ever losing their dignity and edge, venturing into territory previously virginal to Chicano artists. Whether pioneering comedy shows on TV, opening for Rage Against the Machine, collaborating with Asian- and African-American comedians, or making videos with independent filmmakers, their message was clear: "We must be everywhere, infect every medium, intrude in every space, irritate everyone democratically—gringos and Latinos, men and women, community centers and the mainstream."

In the past seven years, their project "Culture Clash in Americca" has attempted to measure the temperature of various cities in the U.S., places where Latino culture protagonizes its most formidable battles and epic dilemmas. From the U.S.-Mexico border to Manhattan, and from San Francisco to Washington D.C., the Clasheros have now become reverse anthropologists and social detectives, researching the trepidatious terrain of interracial relations beyond Chicanismo.

What sets Culture Clash apart from most comedy troupes is that their original material happens also to be good performance literature. This, their second book, is a good example of the work of three important artist-writers who also happen to make us laugh a lot.

Guillermo Gómez-Peña *is an award-winning artist-writer and the author of* Warrior for Gringostroika.

Introduction

By Tony Taccone

I first saw Culture Clash some twenty years ago, in a tiny club tucked into some back alley of San Francisco's Mission District. There was no ventilation in the place, a fact made starkly real by the teeming crowd, while the splinters protruding from the rickety chairs were the stuff of medieval torture. But the young audience, composed entirely of Latinos in those days, was brimming with excitement; any sense of inconvenience was obliterated by their hunger to see the Clash.

It soon became clear why. Richard Montoya, Ric Salinas and Herbert Siguenza took the stage with the swagger and bravura of a righteous rock band. The skits they performed that night were full of spit and vinegar: they skewered the bloated racism of the Right, the pomposity of the Left and almost everyone else in between, including themselves. They made fun of stoners and CEOs, beaners and white trash, black, brown, yellow, red . . . the full rainbow laid wide open for relentless, satiric dissection. To top it off, they managed to pull off this outrageous lampooning while somehow making everyone present feel damn good about it. Especially themselves. It was an impressive if not astonishing feat of comic deprecation-celebration.

Twenty years later, and the boys are still rockin' the house. Except now (dare I say?) they've matured. Not in the sense of having "toned down the act" or having tailored their material to conventional aesthetic mores. Such actions would have killed the essential spirit of their work, compromised the enormous size of their souls and quickly relegated them to the dustbin of history. No, if anything, the energy of their performances over the years has only increased, along with the size and makeup of the crowds.

The maturity that I speak of developed from a consciously articulated desire to raise the level of their art. They wanted to create a body of material that more fully captured that vast and complex phenomena called "the modern American consciousness." They sought a deeper understanding of racism, not just quick character snapshots that poked fun at a particular statement or behavior, but layered portraits and scenes that expressed the complexity and contradiction of people's attitudes and lives. Like amateur detectives obsessed with unlocking a great mystery, they set out to uncover pieces of personal and collective history.

Armed with these lofty aims, the Clash embarked upon a ten-year artistic journey that focused on interviews conducted with hundreds of people from every walk of American life. From Miami to L.A., from New York to San Francisco, from Seattle to D.C., they scoured ghetto streets and city halls, back alley bars and suburban tract homes, RV parks and high-rise offices. They spoke with people of every race, creed and color: the young and the old, the rich and the poor, with those whose families have lived in this country for generations to recently arrived immigrants . . . the collection of stories is remarkable for its variety and style.

Taken together, the result is nothing less than an entertaining, engrossing and, sometimes disturbing, portrait of America: a testament to the fact that our racial attitudes are folded deep within a collective psyche and expressed by the weirdest range of human behaviors and situations. A Haitian man who respects Castro has a son who idolizes Snoop Dogg; aging radicals from San Francisco bemoan the gentrification of their city while getting stoned out of their minds; an ex-Marine compares race relations to dogs screwing in the street; three cons describe the hierarchy of hate behind prison walls; a street poet in a park wails a song of despair and hope, of limitation and longing–the promise of freedom combined with hard reality that defines life in America.

The fact that the material is presented in such a creative and funny manner, as well as being serious and complex, is a testament to the collective talent, intelligence and confidence of Culture Clash. Montoya, Salinas and Siguenza have given us a body of work that truly reaches a diverse audience; one that explores topical ideas not only as a way of satirizing current events but as a way of capturing those elusive human paradigms deemed universal.

Moreover, they have given us a model for success. Against all odds and amidst every conceivable pressure, from the lure of Hollywood to the differing needs of three individual (aging!) men, they made an astonishing commitment: to stick together— through sickness and health, for richer or poorer, for better or worse, Culture Clash keeps singing, keeps dancing, keeps laughing, giving us an ever-expanding body of plays that feeds our heads and hearts. May we all keep the faith with them.

Tony Taccone *is the Artistic Director of Berkeley Repertory Theatre in Berkeley, California.*

Bordertown

SAN DIEGO & TIJUANA

ACKNOWLEDGMENTS

Culture Clash thanks the following people—without them this project would have been impossible: Raffas and Los Cabrones Motorcycle Club, Chunky y los Alacranes, Tribal Gear, Salvador "Queso" Torres, Gloria Torres, The McCulloughs, Ozzie Smith, CECUT, Sheriff Kolander, Gilbert Castellanos, Victor Ochoa, Mario Torero, El Centro Cultural de la Raza, Chicano Park, Victor Payan, Zarco Guerrero, Southwestern College, Bill Virchis, Mr. and Mrs. Rafael Garibay, Frea, Macedonio and Teatro Itzcalli, Nora and Eric Kessler and Shamu.

Introduction to BORDERTOWN

By Sam Woodhouse

Anthropological/artistic/detective work in San Diego and Tijuana is more than a bipolar experience. San Diego is a collection of small towns with a brand-new downtown, wrestling with the newly discovered consciousness of becoming America's seventh largest city. Tijuana is described by the young Tijuanense architect Raúl Cárdenas Osuna as "a new urban culture that makes an improvisation of everything America throws away." Both cities are chock-full of immigrants and entrepreneurs, people who have come out west or up north in search of a new chance.

The particular investigative work of Culture Clash in my part of the world led the trio to sleepy beach towns — the memories of Navy boys straight and gay; Adelita's in Tijuana's Zona Rosa, where the maquiladora janitor dances with the schoolteacher moonlighting as a club girl; a park under a concrete bridge with the nation's most political collection of La Raza murals; and the naturalization center in the neighborhood of City Heights where seventy-seven dialects and thirty-four languages are spoken daily.

Despite hours on the streets, in the homes and by the water, Culture Clash was a bit stumped in a search for the "heart" of this binational region. "Is there a *here* here?" was a seminal and leading question. When we announced the title of this new play about our region, many people asked me, "Where is *Border-town?*"

There is nothing quite so satisfying for a home-grown artistic director than to help make a play about his hometown—a region with an impressive catalog of political and psychological borders and boundaries. Mexicans have a saying about their country in relation to the United States that roughly translates: "So close and yet so far from God." Many Mexicans are terrified that the awesome seductive onslaught of American consumer culture will forever change that which is truly Mexican. Many gringos secretly worry that immigration from the south will forever change the culture they are proud to call "American."

The production of *Bordertown* was many things to many people: an eye-opener to those who only see themselves in the mirror, a long-deserved chance to be heard for the insistent, a lesson in diversity for all of us and, most of all, a response by three brilliant and curious artists to this unique part of the world.

One evening after a performance at San Diego Repertory Theatre, Culture Clash was hosting a very opinionated, funny and divisive "talk back" with the audience. I noticed a *very* blond woman in the back row struggling to raise her hand through the tears that were pouring down her face. When I asked her why she was crying, through her tears she blurted out, "Because I never knew that this place I live in is so damn interesting!"

I never met Peer Gynt, but as a native San Diegan I can speak for many of us here on the border and say, "Thank you, Clash, for peeling our onion."

Sam Woodhouse *is the Artistic Director of San Diego Repertory Theatre.*

PRODUCTION HISTORY

Bordertown was commissioned by San Diego Repertory Theatre (Sam Woodhouse, Artistic Director; John Redman, Managing Director), where it premiered in the summer of 1998. The director was Sam Woodhouse; the scenic and costume design was by Christopher Acebo, the sound design was by Randy Cohen and Pea Hicks, the lighting design was by Jeff Rowlings; the visual consultant was David Avalos, the choreographer was Paula Present, the dramaturg was Nakissa Etemand and the stage manager was Alexis Randolph.

Act 1

The Metropolis

Blackness. Sound of crickets. Someone whistles a signal. We hear the sound of a speeding truck come to a screeching stop. A door slams.

Militia Man: Halt! Halt!

(We hear panicked voices in Spanish.)

Mexicans: Córrale! Córrale!

(People are running. The "truck lights" sweep the stage and the audience left to right. A shotgun blast.
Lights up. Two Mexican illegals are caught, frozen like deer in the harsh lights. The Militia Man in head-to-toe army fatigues has captured them. The Mexicans, wearing cowboy hats and boots, are frantic yet they fully comply with the armed Militia Man who leads them toward center stage.
A coyote howls in the distance. We are deep in eastern San Diego County.)

Militia Man: Alto! Alto! Hold still.
Mexican 1 and 2: Señor, no somos Mexicanos, está equivocado. Por favor . . .
Militia Man *(Pointing his shotgun at their heads)*: Shut up! Get down on your knees. ¡Abajo! Put your hands behind your back.

(The two men comply.)

Mexican 1: We're not Mexicans, sir.
Militia Man: Just hush up now!
Mexican 2: But we're not Mexicans, mister.
Militia Man: I said, shut the fuck up! Just pipe down, godammit.

(The Militia Man speaks into his walkie-talkie.)

Delta Foxtrot, this is Chainsaw Civilian Volunteer 1-8-7, come in. I got two wets, over.
Mexican 1: We are not wetbacks, sir!
Militia Man: I said, shut the fuck up!

(Mexican 2 begins to get up.)

Hey, where you think you're goin'? Get down! ¡Abajo! ¡Abajo! You wanna cap in your ass, boy?
Mexican 2: No, sir.
Militia Man *(Into walkie-talkie)*: Yeah, got a little problem here . . . I'm approximately three clicks east of the canal. Location, Maupin Ranch. Gonna wait for the Border Patrol to pick these boys up. Possible drug runners, over.
Mexican 2: We are not drug runners, mister!
Militia Man *(Cocking the shotgun)*: Hey, I said, cállate la boca, comprende?
Mexican 1: He doesn't speak Spanish, sir. He's a Chicano!
Militia Man: Very funny, just save it for the Border Patrol when they get here.

(The Militia Man uses the shotgun to nudge their backpacks closer to him. He starts looking through them.)

Mexican 1: If you look in our backpacks there, you will find our passports, driver's license, sun block . . . We're Americans, sir.
Militia Man: That don't mean shit. Got any weapons, pistolas?
Mexican 1 and 2: No, sir.
Militia Man: You got any drugs in here?

(The Mexicans look at each other not sure.)

Mexican 1 and 2: Uhmm . . . no, sir.

Militia Man: Don't lie to me now, because if you lie to me, you know what's gonna happen here, tell me the truth . . .

(The Militia Man finds a small tape recorder inside the backpack.)

Aha! Found something. Who'd you roll for this gadget? What is this for?

Mexican 1: It's a tape recorder. We use that for our interviews.

Militia Man: What interviews?

Mexican 1: We're a theater group. We're interviewing Mexican nationals for our play about San Diego and Tijuana . . .

Mexican 2: You know, the people, the voices, their hopes, their dreams, maybe a song or two . . .

Militia Man: Shut the fuck up! Now let's see what this says . . .

(The Militia Man presses the play button on the recorder. A voice speaking in Spanish is heard.)

Voice On Tape: ¡El gobernador de California, Pete Wilson, me puede besar el culo! Ha, ha, ha!

(The Militia Man turns off the tape.)

Militia Man: What the hell was that? What else you got in here?

(The Militia Man pulls out papers from the backpacks.)

Let's see . . . *(Reading)* "The San Diego Repertory Theatre Rehearsal Schedule." What the hell?

Mexican 2: We're actors. Equity, Lort D.

Militia Man: You know, they do a real nice *Christmas Carol* there. I go with the missus every year.

Mexican 1: Are you a subscriber, sir?

Militia Man: You damned right.

Mexican 2: Great, a subscriber with a gun. August Wilson was right!

Militia Man: Who's August Wilson?

Mexican 2: Just another Mexican national we interviewed back on the ridge.

Militia Man: Well, I better not catch him in my area, that's all I'm saying . . .

(The Militia Man finds a parking pass inside the backpacks.)

What the hell is this? *(Reading)* "Horton Plaza Mall Monthly Parking Pass?" Hell, I can't even afford one of these! They have to be stolen. Alright boys, you have to prove something to me. What level do you park on in Horton Plaza Mall?

Mexican 2: What level?

Militia Man: What level do you park on?

(He points the shotgun at them.)

Mexican 2: Level Three!

Militia Man: No!

Mexican 1: Level Four?

Militia Man: Aha! I gotcha now!

Mexican 2: Avocado!

Militia Man: What's Level Five?

Mexican 1: Onion!

Militia Man: Level Six?

Mexican 1: Tomato!

Militia Man: Level Seven?

Mexican 2: Kiwi!

Militia Man: Level Eight?

Mexican 1 and 2: Kumquat!

Militia Man: Shit! You *must* be Americans! Hell, I gotta turn you loose. I was gonna break my record. I caught thirty-eight mojados this month already. You two would have made forty. I could have won the Swiss Army knife set, damn it!

(The Militia Man lowers his shotgun. The Mexicans start putting their possessions back into their backpacks.)

Mexican 2: Sorry we couldn't help you out, sir. But it's good to set goals for yourself none the less.

Mexican 1: Thank you for letting us go. We're as American as apple pie—go Chargers!

Militia Man: The Chargers suck.

Mexican 2: Let's get the fuck out of here.

Mexican 1: Yeah, let's go.

(The Mexicans prepare to leave. They stop in their tracks when they hear the cocking of the Militia Man's shotgun.)

Militia Man: Wait a minute, where do you think you're going?

Mexican 1: We're leaving, we're Americans remember? We have to go interview . . . uh, who do we have to interview?

Mexican 2: Shamu, the whale.

Mexican 1: Yeah, Shamu!

Militia Man: Shamu, my ass! I wanna be interviewed. Put that tape recorder on.

Mexican 2: Sir, this is illegal. You can't hold us like this. Besides, I'm not interested in interviewing Rambo subscriber with a gun who probably saw *Forever Plaid* ten times.

Militia Man: Twelve times! Now turn that son of a bitch on! I got something to say!

(He slowly lifts the shotgun at them.)

Mexican 1 and 2: Right away, sir.

(The Mexicans turn on the tape recorder and sit down.)

Militia Man: First, let me say this, I am an American.

Mexican 2: Fine.

Militia Man: I have the right to bear arms.

Mexican 2: Fine.

Militia Man: I have the right to defend my country.

Mexican 2: Excellent interview. Thanks.

(The Mexicans turn off the tape recorder.)

Militia Man: I'm not finished! Now sit down! I am only upholding the law in the absence of law enforcement.

Mexican 2: You must be tight with the Border Patrol?

Militia Man: Most of the Border Patrol officers I know are Tejanos, Mexican-Americans, damn good law men too.

(Militia Man takes a knee.)

See, back in the day we would have one or two Mexicans coming through here a day. Now days, you got twenty, thirty wets a day for Christ's sakes. Looks like a goddamn 10K run. They got no respect for the land, they defecate in the open, they tear down the fences, steal animals, they shoot at each other. There's been two killings, Santería, Chupacabra tortures, rapings. You name it, we got it.
(Pointing off into the distance) See that?

Mexican 1: What is that?

Militia Man: That, my amigo, is a dead coyote hanging upside down. I call her Fluffy.

Mexican 1: Why is it there?

Mexican 2: To discourage coyotes of the human kind.

Militia Man: Yep, Mexicans are a superstitious lot. It's like the wild west out here, a little law and order is needed. Now, this ranch here belongs to Mrs. Wescott . . . But uh, please don't use her real name.

Mexican 2 *(Taking notes on a pad)*: Is that one "T" or two?

Militia Man: Two Ts. Anyway, she would hire the wetbacks. They would work the ranch and teach ol' lady Wescott things like how to make medicinal teas from wild cacti, how best to slaughter livestock, and so on, have a chance to make a little dinero before they continued north. It was a great arrangement for everyone. But if you ask me, after NAFTA, the whole goddamn thing fell apart!

Mexican 2: What fell apart, sir?

Militia Man: The liberal do-gooders protested "light up the border,"* Clinton was a pussy with the corrupt bastards in the Mexican government, the Narco Traficantes are too dan-

---

* A movement by citizens who would light the border with their car headlights.

gerous, so the wets move east. And here we are, East San Diego County, gateway to the Great White North.

Mexican 2: Let me get this straight, you're not a Border Patrol officer, you're not military—so that makes you a vigilante.

Militia Man: I've been called worse.

Mexican 2: Have you ever had to shoot or kill someone?

Militia Man: I shot at a couple of guys, don't know if I killed them or not.

Mexican 2: How do you feel about the militarization of the border?

Militia Man: The what?

Mexican 2: Global economy as it affects the border?

Militia Man: The hell you say . . .

Mexican 2: You must of heard about the boy shot dead in Texas by Marines, they left his body in a irrigation ditch . . .

Militia Man: The Mexican boy?

Mexican 2: No. He was an American, sir.

Militia Man: He was Mexican!

(The Militia Man walks away. Mexican 2 follows him.)

Mexican 2: Ezequiel Hernández was an American who looked like a Mexican. He was an American. I'm an American . . . *(Pointing at Mexican 1)* He's an American . . .

Militia Man: I've heard enough . . .

Mexican 2: Now hold on here. We listened to you. *(Takes out files from his backpack)* I have nearly three hundred cases right here sir, all documented, factual border abuse cases of people detained in cells for five days without water. Border Patrol agents abusing and detaining U.S. citizens because they looked Mexican, that was their crime, looking like a Mexican!

Militia Man: They could have been terrorists!

Mexican 2: I never heard of a Mexican national blowing up a federal building.

Militia Man: The hell . . .

Mexican 2: Why do you do this, sir? I'd really like to know. I mean aside from the patriotic shit, why do you dress up like Rambo and patrol the border?

Mexican 1 *(Worried)*: Dude, be cool!
Mexican 2: No, fuck this, I'd really like to know.

(The Militia Man contemplates the question.)

Militia Man: Truth is, I'm scared . . .
Mexican 2: You got all the guns, man!
Mexican 1: Hey man be cool.
Militia Man: I'm sacred for my daughter, my country. I have the right to be scared don't I?
Mexican 2: I don't know, I'd have to read the Constitution . . .

(The Militia Man loses his composure, takes out his hand revolver and puts it against the head of Mexican 2.)

Militia Man: The Constitution don't mean ass-wipe out here, Pancho.
Mexican 2: OK man, please don't . . .

(The crackle of the walkie-talkie breaks the tense moment.)

Walkie-Talkie Voice: "Chainsaw, come in, over."
Militia Man: Ah shit!

(The Militia Man puts his revolver away and answers the call.)

Chainsaw, here. Roger that, I'll be right there, over and out. We got twenty wets who just broke through the south ridge. It's a mile away, gotta hump . . .

(The Militia Man is about to leave. Suddenly, a loud spacecraft sound builds. There is a sharp shaft of light from above. Everyone hits the deck. The spacecraft "flies over" and is gone.)

What the hell was that? Must be one of the Patrol's new Apache birds. Gotta go.
Mexican 1: Do you mind telling us your name, sir?
Militia Man: Frederick S. Ward.
Mexican 1: What does the "S" stand for?
Mexican 2: Shit-kicker.

Militia Man: Shit-kicker. Ha, ha, ha. You're really funny, boy. *(Points his shotgun for the final time)* You should be a comedian.

(The Mexicans share a weary chuckle.)

Well, gotta run. SEMPER VIGILANCE!

(The Militia Man exits into the night. The Mexicans look at each other.)

Mexican 1: That was a trip, dude.
Mexican 2: Oh god he's coming back!

(The Militia Man darts back in, trying to catch his breath.)

Militia Man: Say, can you boys get me some *Christmas Carol* tickets?

(The Militia Man exits quickly. A coyote is heard in the distance.)

Mexican 2 *(Into tape recorder):* Note to self. Two house seats for Mr. and Mrs. Shit-kicker. *(Clicks off recorder)*

(The Mexicans take a final look around.)

This place is fucking weird.

(Blackout. Radio montage transition of real San Diego and Tijuana radio stations. We hear futuristic space music. An intense Bald Man wearing a purple cosmic gown and Nike sneakers appears center stage.)

Bald Man: Greetings, Earthlings. There are no borders in the cosmos, only infinitesimal possibilities. No one really dies; you just change frequency. The body disintegrates because it is made of atomic, earthly elements. However, our mind is a fourth-dimensional energy system. Transcending space and time, where there is no beginning or ending. We become in tune with the infinite. This is our higher self.

Therefore, prepare to escape from San Diego and leave behind your personal, cultural and political borders. Journey with us to the borderless cosmos, where race, creed and religion does not matter . . .

(Lights and cosmic sounds fade. Marilyn Manson's "Beautiful People" is heard. A young man dressed in black goth attire enters on a skateboard.)

Goth Guy: I tried to leave San Diego, twice, but there's a weird gravity that pulls you back.

(He starts to paint his nails black.)

It's like the gravitational force that the beach or the bahía would have. San Diego tries to be bohemian but it cannot. San Francisco has that all done. In fact, anyone who has bohemian sensibilities here is gone; as soon as they turn eighteen, they're gone.

San Diego has its idiosyncrasies; people come to see exactly what they came to see, they don't want to be surprised. They want to know exactly what it is they came to see; if it's different, they say, "I'm very disappointed that I didn't see what I came for; not what I expected."

San Diego is the seventh largest city in the country, but it has an inferiority complex. Los Angeles has the cultural magnetism of the music and film industries and San Diego will always be in the shadow of that. And culturally it is very confused. Once San Diego embraces the indigenous nature of where it is, and it realizes that with Tijuana it can be one of the greater metropolises on the Pacific Rim, it'll take off, and until it does that, it will continue to gyrate in its own ghosts.

(Goth Guy skates off. We hear breezy, soft jazz. A rich La Jolla Woman enters dressed in a matching workout jumpsuit, drinking Evian water.)

La Jolla Woman: When I first moved to La Jolla, they wouldn't allow Jews to live here in La Jolla or in Rancho Santa Fe. Isn't that awful? *(Beat)* Oh, I heard a good joke the other day, my friend is a Catholic, and at her parish here in La Jolla, when the priest was serving the wine, the congregation sent it back for a better year! Ha, ha, ha. Isn't that charming? *(To someone offstage)* Julia! Where's my coffee? *(To herself)* Just can't get good "help" anymore.

(Her Maid Julia enters. She hands La Jolla Woman her coffee. The Maid exits carrying a basket of dirty clothes. Her face is never seen.)

Generally, what I am is a community volunteer. Well, I volunteer because I'm not going to stay home and play bridge or go shopping all day. It's more interesting. I get to see different cultures that way. And boy, do we have tons of culture here, but it's a strange mix. A hodgepodge. I call it a "Callaloo." Do you know what that is? That's a West Indian stew that has spices and herbs, but you can still taste all the individual flavors. It's quite delicious. City Heights is a great example; my husband hates it when I go there, but they say there are twenty-three different languages spoken there. It's the Ellis Island of the '90s. And San Diego better realize that's the future of this city.

(The Maid walks by with a basket of folded clothes. Again her face is not seen.)

They call it "America's finest city," but quite frankly I'm worried about San Diego, and what I recently experienced. People were telling me to go home! They were saying a white woman of fifty-six can't have anything to do or say about problems that face a certain neighborhood. Now this made me really sad. It was terrible. I tried to bring a little order to their meetings, because quite frankly a lot of people didn't know how to function around a table. People yelling and screaming, arguing, and accusing each other. But to tell me to go home, it hurt my feelings. I don't think I can fix their problems but there are a lot of people like me who can help out with ideas, communication skills, resources. I'm only trying to give a little help, not a lot. So, I went home, I had to go home.

(Blackout. A shaft of bright light reveals the silhouette of a girl, Julia. We never see her face. She carries a laundry basket. We hear helicopter sounds in the distance.)

Julia: To cross the border is a big decision, it's like being reborn. I never walk so much in my life. Two days to cross. Not just one mountain, but mountain after mountain. In the day I was so hot and thirsty, it hurt to swallow. At night I was so scared. I couldn't see in front of me and I kept falling down. My feet were bleeding. I had to keep up with the men. And it was so cold, I couldn't stop shaking. We almost make it, but they catch us. And they were so rough; they pull out guns; they push us and call us bad names. They deport us back to Mexicali.

We called our mamá. She live in San Diego. We cry to her on the telephone. She say to us, no try to cross again. But the next day we try again, again it took two days, more walking, all those mountains, six miles of mountains, but this time we make it across! Cruzamos el cerco. I never forget the look on my mamá's face when we surprise her. We hug and cry. I'll never forget that day, it was my quinceñera, my fifteen-year birthday.

We not know anyone here in San Diego. But we meet a group that help and accept us. They made us feel wanted here. We joined the Mormons. Dios mio, it was so funny when we got baptized! My brothers, sisters, y mamá, all of us dressed in white. We looked like angels. We had to hold our laughter. We were reborn. You know that big white Mormon temple, the one in La Jolla, the one that looks like a spaceship? One day they let us go inside.

(Lights fade out on Julia. Lights come up on an elderly Chinese Man in classic leisure wear as he prepares to tee off on one of the region's countless private golf courses.)

Chinese Man: My father migrated to San Diego in 1914. He was sixteen years old then. Not knowing English, the first place he went to, was a Presbyterian mission in the old China-town area, around 3rd and J streets. There, they clothed him, fed him and taught him English. He was impressed with the Bible story of David and Goliath, and being such a small guy himself, he adopted the Biblical name of David. He later became a fruit peddler, and named it David's Fruit and Produce. Then he opened a wholesale produce house and called it David's Produce Company. And then he started packing peaches and can goods and called it David's Brands. So everything he did was called David. When I was a little boy, I remember people came up and said, "How in the world did a Chinese family get a name like that?"

The Chinese started the fishing business here in San Diego, but they were forced out of it, because in 1882 Congress passed an exclusion law. So when the Chinese took their boats out beyond the two-mile limit, the law said that technically they had left the country. And when they came back, they said that they had entered illegally. It was one way to exclude Chinese from emigrating into the United States and to stop them from fishing. This exclusion law was the first and only law passed by Congress naming a specific people.

The first occasion when I realized the social differences here in San Diego was when we saved enough money to buy a bigger house. We found a house, but the broker told us that the owner didn't want to sell it to us because we were Chinese. There was a racial covenant law. The deed restriction said that only Caucasians could buy. I couldn't understand that; we had the money. That was my first encounter of social injustice. Maybe that was some incentive for me to become a real estate broker.

During the '60s, I was in public office for many years. I was the first minority ever elected to the City Council. But I remember when I started running, my opponent's campaign headquarters had a sign with a quote: TOM DOESN'T HAVE A CHINAMAN'S CHANCE. "A Chinaman's chance," that's an old phrase that goes back to the goldmine days, when the Chinese really didn't have a chance, because whatever they got into, they would pass laws against them.

No, I'm not retired; I just find more time for golf. I play golf in Balboa Park or Torrey Pines. San Diego County has over a hundred golf courses. Next week we're going to Baja Mar, which is next to Ensenada, with my son David. He's a real good golfer. I don't have a "Chinaman's Chance" to beat him. Ha, ha, ha.

(Finally, the Chinese Man swings at the ball.)

Fore!!

(Blackout. Lights come up on a man dimly lit, standing in the shadows. We hear a voice intone:)

Poway, Vista, San Marcos, Encinitas, Del Mar, Lemon Grove, Santee, Solana Beach, Imperial Beach.

(Lights quickly up on the office of the Sheriff of San Diego County.)

Sheriff: I've got seven jails, the sixth largest jail in the country. And of course, when you talk of this region, you have to talk about the busiest international border in the world. Here's a little heads-up for you, back in the '60s when I was a kid, you would have five to ten thousand border crossings a year, both legal and illegal, now you got 4.5 million a month, 4.5 million Mexicans and Americans going back and forth. That's a whole lot of people coming into California every month. You know what it is I think? "It's the cheese!"

(The Sheriff has a good laugh.)

I thought you might appreciate that. Now we are not in the business of capturing Mexicans, but I can tell you this, our jails are full of dangerous felons who are here illegally.

Look, I'm just a Jewish kid from Chicago, I'm lucky to be here. I don't take myself seriously but I do take my job seriously. I was the Chief of Police from '75 to '88. I worked at the *Union Tribune* for three years—crazy job.

I have a zero tolerance for racism in the department and I am very proud about that. We have deputies in all the unincorporated areas of San Diego, we got wildlife in the county, and as of five years ago, we got plenty of Cripps and Bloods as well.

Because the region is so heavily interracial, it brings up special problems. When I was Police Chief, the federal government brought in nearly twenty thousand Vietnamese, Laotians and Cambodians into the Linda Vista area alone. I don't think I'm exaggerating here but there are four different languages spoken, the customs are different, as a result we have domestic situations like: ". . . Uh, where's my cat, where's my dog?" 9-1-1 was flooded with "Where's Fluffy?" calls. You may laugh, and shame on you, but where these people came from, that was normal. Where these people came from, they didn't trust the cops. Where these people came from, the cops would kill them and their family. And that just doesn't happen here in San Diego.

(An Office Aid enters.)

Office Aid: Press Conference at 0-700, sir.
Sheriff: Thanks Bob. How about that weather?
Office Aid: How about that Viagra?
Sheriff: Hoo-wa!

(The Office Aid takes a file from the Sheriff and walks across the stage. He hands the file to a Reporter, who has been sitting in the shadows opposite the Sheriff, then exits. Lights up on the Reporter.)

Reporter: Is there an incident that stands out in my mind? Hmm . . . Yeah. Tyrone Thomas . . . Case #7734. I was a cub reporter on the police beat. It involved a black kid named Tyrone. Tyrone Thomas. Tyrone was a little junkie. The cops made him their flunky, their snitch. One day, Tyrone is on the street. Two cops see him and decide to shake him down. Tyrone, for whatever reason, sees the cops and decides he don't want to deal with them that day, so he runs into this hotel, this very notorious junkie hotel, called the Ebony Inn. Now, the Ebony Inn has this courtyard with only two entrances, one cop blocks one entrance, and the other cop blocks the other. They got Tyrone caged in. Now, one cop has his gun drawn, and the other cop has his gun out and his nightstick. The cops say, "Tyrone, give it up and come on over here." Now, Tyrone walks over to the cop with the nightstick, but he makes a break for it, trying to run past the cop. Now, Tyrone is a small-time junkie, no weapon, plus the cops knew him. Now the cop tries to subdue him with the nightstick, and instead of putting the gun back in the holster, the officer hits Tyrone over the head with the revolver. He hits him so hard, that the gun fires.

(We hear the sound of a single gunshot.)

Blows his brains out. All right? Kills the kid.

(Pause.)

And for me, god, this was back in '78, yeah, '78. I'm forty-six now, I must've been twenty-eight, not much older than Tyrone, and I'm thinking, wow, this is BS. You know? The thing was that this was an accident mainly because of the way this cop thought about black people; he just wanted to give Tyrone a good old-fashion pistol whipping. And the thing I kept asking myself is, Why not use the nightstick? And where could Tyrone have gone? They had him boxed in, bordered in. I have walked that scene a million times, in my mind, and in that courtyard. If this had been a white kid, would this terrible accident have happened? People knew I was excited about this issue. And this story blew up real big. And it got really ugly. And to this day there are still conflicting stories about that kid. I just wanted justice for Tyrone. Who cries for Tyrone the junkie? Killed in the Ebony Inn courtyard? Tyrone came face to face with the powers that be in an indirect and tragic way. Tyrone Thomas. God bless him, you know? I eventually had to get off the police beat because I couldn't distinguish the good guys from the bad guys!

(From the other side of the stage the Sheriff chimes in.)

Sheriff: Tyrone Thomas? It's been so long. I'd have to check the file . . .

(Lights up on Ozzie.)

Ozzie: Now what are you guys going to do with this stuff, man? You know, I'm a black man living in San Diego. What do you expect me to say, man? Am I getting set up here? Did the sheriff send you guys? Now, what's the name of your group? Culture Bash? Culture Crash? Ha, ha, ha . . .

(Lights down on Ozzie.)

Sheriff: Tyrone Thomas? That case jogs the memory. I don't recall, I'll have to check the microfilm on that one. But as far as the events that stand out in my mind? Good question: September 25, 1978, North Park the PSA crash; July 19, 1984, James Huberty walks into McDonald's in San Ysidro, California, and kills twenty-two people. Now I was the first one to go in there, and let me tell you, it was far worse than the PSA crash. At the PSA crash in North Park, you weren't quite sure of what you were looking at, but in San Ysidro that day, my god, you had the sixteen-year-old kid behind the counter, grandmother and grandfather taking their little granddaughter for her Happy Meal. But twenty-four people walked out of there alive; we're very proud of that. It took us forty minutes to figure out what was going on, how many hostages, how many gunmen. As soon as we could ascertain the situation, we fired a single shot—

(A single gunshot is heard.)

Killed Huberty instantly. Even though everybody killed that day were Latino, I don't believe in my heart that it was a hate crime. James Huberty was a crazy person. According to his wife's testimony, he woke up that morning and said, "Today I'm gonna kill something," and by golly he did.

You know, the McDonald's massacre and the PSA crash, these events as tragic and unspeakable as they were did not define us as a city—random acts of savagery and violence happen anywhere, anytime. Look at Oklahoma City, the schoolyard in Arkansas, even Andrew Cunanan for that matter.

The Heaven's Gate mass suicide situation in Rancho Santa Fe will be much more difficult to deflect as a city. These crazy people came here to our region, to our paradise, and did their terrible deed here. I'm afraid the rest of the country might be looking at San Diego as a place for kooks and nuts.

(The Sheriff pulls out a Nike tennis shoe in an evidence bag. He holds it up and looks at it.)

This may define us.

(There is a photo flash. Slow fade to black. We hear the dirge of African ceremonial music. The Sheriff exits.

Lights change. A Muslim Woman wearing a black burqa enters center stage. She is slowly and methodically followed by a second and then a third Woman, all wearing black burqas. The three move with slow and determined movements. Their dance is ritualistic; it slowly builds to a climax.

In an instant, the lights change. The burqas fall to the ground, revealing three sailors in white Navy uniforms. We hear military marching drums. The sailors march. After a moment they stand at attention.)

Chicano Navy Guy: Attention!

(The three sailors salute stiffly.)

Liberty, boys!

(We hear Frank Sinatra's "South of the Border." The sailors toss their swabbie hats in the air and dance in a choreographed manner typical of movie musicals of the 1950s. The music stops.)

1951. Chicanos in the Navy. We came to San Diego, most of us were children of farm-working parents from the San Joaquin Valley, little farm towns like Fowler, Selma and Sanger up around Fresno. We came prepared to deal with how we were going to be perceived as Chicanos. The Zoot Suit riots were still fresh in our minds, so were the Japanese internment camps. And the way blacks had been treated in the South braced us for the worst. But when you saw the lights of San Diego shimmer at night for the first time, even from your barracks—man you couldn't wait for your two-hour pass y ya te chingaron!

(1950s swing music.)

We kept our civies at the Seven Seas Locker Club and we were off. Waves of swabbies in their Navy blues, our hats bobbing up and down like a conveyer belt on Market Street.
   Hey guys, let's go to the Balboa!
Black Navy Guy: How about the Tower Theater?
White Navy Guy: Nah, the Cabrillo!
Chicano Navy Guy: The Spreckels!
Black Navy Guy: No, the Orpheum!
White Navy Guy: The Fox!
Chicano Navy Guy: How about the Mexican Movie house at the end of 5th Street?
White and Black Navy Guy: Nah . . .
Chicano Navy Guy: There was the Famous Door with great-looking hostesses who all lived on Ash and 5th Street.

(They all whistle.)

White Navy Guy: Hey Montoya, let's go down to TJ and catch that comic named Johnny Hotnuts!

Black Navy Guy: No, let's go pick up some señoritas at La Bamba.

Chicano and White Navy Guy: Yeah, La Bamba!

Chicano Navy Guy: La Bamba was a notorious Chicano bar in the Logan, the barrio. Now the last thing you wanted to do was walk in there with a bunch of white Navy guys. We had to find a way to distance ourselves from our black buddies too. They didn't take us to their bars on El Cajon or La Jolla. There was an uncomfortableness when they came with us. Now these guys were our buddies, don't get me wrong, and my old gringo buddy from Texas, he would be the first to go down when the shit hit the fan!

(White and Black Navy Guy throw a couple of blows with each other. The Chicano Navy Guy gets between them and breaks it up.)

C'mon vatos!

White Navy Guy: He started it, the goddamned Negro!

Black Navy Guy: Fuck you, Okie!

Chicano Navy Guy: There goes the pinche neighborhood!

(They all laugh. Ocean sounds are heard.)

I was assigned to the USS *Dextrose*, a mine sweeper. My captain was a great old guy who would take target practice on the bow of the ship shooting at rare albatrosses with his shotgun.

(Shotgun blast. The White Captain enters.)

White Captain: Goddammit! I missed the son of a bitch!

Chicano Navy Guy: Better luck next time, sir. My captain took a liking to me. He let me cook huevos rancheros every Sunday morning in the galley, as long as we gave him some. He would say things to me like . . .

White Captain: Montoya! You're gonna sink this goddamned boat!

Chicano Navy Guy: I'm trying my best, sir!

(Chicano Navy Guy salutes the White Captain. The White Captain exits.)

Chicanos knew how to modify our uniforms just right. We had to look cool, not culo sabes? Shape the hat. Make the bells wider, tie the boots just so, the Airborne stole that from us.

Black and White Navy Guy: Fuckin' jar heads!

Chicano Navy Guy: We always wore hard shoes, never the gook shoes most guys wore. The chicks liked that classy look. We got that from our Pachuco big brothers.

All: Orale!

(All three strike a Pachuco pose.)

Chicano Navy Guy: Say fellas, when I get out of the Navy I'm trying to get a scholarship to art school, but for now I'm gonna go to City College on the G.I. Bill! My wife Mary Ellen is going to have our first child, and guess what fellas? I have a job waiting for me in National City!

All: National fuckin' City!!!!

(They hoop and holler.)

White Navy Guy: The number one mission when you got off the ship was to get laid.

(James Brown's "It's a Man's Man's Man's World" is heard. The Chicano and Black Navy Guy fall out several feet upstage of the White Navy Guy.)

It was like, "Where did you go last night and did you get any?" Back in the '70s there were a lot of sailor bars, peep shows, locker clubs, right there along Broadway—clubs where you could pick up girls. Every night had a different scene at different places: bands, single women, lots of socializing. And more often than not, nobody scored, it was a lot of bravado. There was always a pursuit to get laid and have a fun time. And I went and had a fun time. The interesting thing about me is, that I'm gay. They didn't know it, but I was in the closet and I played along. I eventually got out of the Navy because it was a crime, it was a federal felony to love a person in the manner that I did.

Chicano Navy Guy: Hey, someone just pinched my ass!

Black Navy Guy: Was that you, Williams?

Chicano Navy Guy: What are ya some sort of faggot, buster?

White Navy Guy: Come on, fellas. Not me!

(They all laugh. The Village People's "In the Navy" is heard. The sailors dance away as the White Navy Guy grabs the butts of the other two sailors. Music fades as the two sailors peel off leaving Black Navy Guy alone onstage.)

Black Navy Guy: In the Navy, you hang out with your own kind and your own rank. There is a hierarchy in the Navy, and the whole military is built on that. There's a chain of command.

When I first came into the Navy, they used to call me "nigger." There was no problem with that. You couldn't mess with them. Especially if it was an officer. The Navy sucks now, it's gone to shit. A chief meant something, now it ain't shit. Too much liberalism, I guess. Women changed it. My commanding officer is a woman. I guess she's the head bitch. And I can't say anything about that. No sir.

Woman *(Voice-over)*: Ensign Johnson, report to the brig. Ensign Johnson.

Black Navy Guy: Shit!

White Navy Guy *(Offstage)*: Did you say something, boy?

(Lights fade on the Black Navy Guy as he stands sadly at attention. He exits.

We hear the classic Chicano anthem "Chicano Park" by Ramon "Chunky" Sanchez and Los Alacranes. Lights up to reveal Chicano artist Cósmico painting a mural. The mood is bright and festive. Chunky, an enormous man with a large mustache and a small guitar, enters carrying a large file folder. He strums his guitar to "Chicano Park." The song fades out. We are at the world-famous Chicano Park in Barrio Logan. Chunky addresses the audience:)

Chunky: Q-vo gente. Welcome to Chicano Park in the heart of San Diego! El Corazón, de Barrio Logan. This crazy vato right here is El Cósmico, muralist, poet, certified barrio-ologist and single father. Sometimes we call him Dr. Moco. Wuzz up, loco?

Cósmico: Hey, Chunky. Aquí no más. Far out vato, just making a sketch for a new mural, tú sabes. Hey Chunky, I got a new poema, man. You want to hear it, aye?

Chunky: Maybe laters ese, I gotta talk to these gentes right now, homes. They're taking a tour of the murals. Gonna give them some historia about the parque and shit.

Cósmico: Orale.

Chunky: Orale.

Cósmico: Orale.

Chunky: Orale

(Putting the bulging file down for a moment.)

Chingao, man, where do I begin? Well you gotta go to the beginning. And for me, personally, because I am a child of farm worker parents, from Blithe, I was able to apply and was accepted to San Diego State in 1970.

(Strobe lights flicker as Jimmy Hendrix's "Purple Haze" blasts for a moment. Cósmico and Chunky dance like far-out hippies. Peobody, a Chicano biker rolls onto the stage on a beautiful Harley Davidson. He wears a vest and mustache, a wallet chain and a black bandanna. Suddenly the music stops and the Harley engine fades out.)

Goddamn, now that was a flashback!

(Chunky makes trails with his hand.)

I saw trails and shit ese! Hey everybody, this is Mr. Peobody right here from Los Cabrones Motorcycle Club. Crazy Locos on Motos. Biklas you know?

Peobody: Q-vo. Did you tell them about the Neighborhood House, Chunky?

Chunky: Not yet, ese, I was gonna get to that.

Cósmico: Hey man, you gotta tell 'em about Queso. Man.

Chunky: Yeah man, I was gonna get to that part, ese.

Cósmico: Don't leave out Queso, man.

Chunky: Chale ese. How you been, Peobody?

Peobody: Not so good ese. The ol' lady, man, she won't let me visit my own kids, man.

Cósmico: You gotta pay the child support ese.

Peobody: I never miss a payment, loco.

Cósmico: That's not what my sister says.

Peobody: Hey, you better watch you say, ese. I'll go Oscar de la Hoya on you!

Chunky: Hey, hey, hey vatos, we can talk about child support later, OK? We'll have a support group and shit. Let's not fight in front of the gringo, this ain't the pinche *Jerry Springer* show. I gotta talk to these gentes right now.

Cósmico: Orale.

Peobody: Orale.

Chunky: Orale. Where was I? 1970. This wasn't even a park then, the Logan was about to explode. This city of San Diego had always shitted on the Logan man, putting junkyards over here, junkyards pa' ya, making the barrio toxic you know? I was involved with Mecha at San Diego State at the time, and on April 22nd at two P.M. in the tarde, we got word that the people were taking over the land. And the word spread like wildfire, man. Chisme is faster than the internet. Little viejitas were out there, our elders, you know, we wanted to stop the bulldozers, the police came out, some people got busted. And that evening, it had made the local news, it really embarrassed the city of San Diego, and then we made the state news, and the national news. I got all the clippings right here, ese. The people of Barrio Logan stood up to the machine, and we stopped them in their tracks.

Cósmico: That's right. Taking over the land, working the land. That was crucial, it wasn't just a party.

Chunky: Hey, that was the first year they had Earth Day, there were a bunch of hippies . . . Do you remember that, ese?

Cósmico: Of course I remember, I married one!

Chunky: Pinche vato married a hippie heina. They got little hippie half-breeds running around. I love those kids like they are my own . . . Hey Cósmico, where's Tonantzín at, ese?

Cósmico: Oh, mija is a Ph.D. student up in Berkeley.

Chunky: And Citlali?

Cósmico: Stanford Law School, ese.

Chunky: And Xichilipotzli?

Cósmico: He's at San Diego City College.

Chunky: You must be really proud of him, huh?

Cósmico *(Disappointed)*: He's in his thirteenth year.

Chunky: ¡Hijole! Well the park got taken over, Centro Cultural got taken over, the Chicano Free Clinic got taken, we burned down a few Taco Bell's . . .

Cósmico: Yeah man, the artista, men and women have always played a key role in the movemiento. So after the park was taken back by the community, Queso, an artista and veterano got this crazy idea to paint murals right on the freeway pillars holding up the Coronado Bridge. So all these different artistas from all over Aztlán got involved. And this collective created this very important work and beautified the barrio at the same time, verdad, Chunky?

Chunky: Simón.

Cósmico: Simón.

Peobody: Simón. But even before the park and the murals and the bridge, Chunky. Don't forget to tell them about the Neighborhood House, man. That was a place where all the different young people could come together with no problemas, there were gangs, not like today though, kids from Snider Continuation School, Sherman, Logan Heights and Shell Town, Los Contes, Los Gatos, the Solteros, The Lobos, The Amigos, Los Gallos, Los Pollos, The Drifters, The Crows, The Sheebas, The Blue Velvets, and the dances at The Coronet, the Metro, Battle of the Bands, fingertip jackets y todo. Everybody felt safe at the Neighborhood House. Don't forget to tell them, Chunky.

Chunky: I think you just did, homes. That was firme, got me right in the corazon. Orale.

Peobody: Orale.

Cósmico: Orale.

Chunky: Can everybody say "orale"?

(The audience responds:)

Audience: Orale!

Chunky: You can all be arrested now for speaking Spanish. One strike for all of you right there.

Cósmico: Hey Chunky, can I read my poem now?

Chunky: Chale man, maybe later aye.

Cósmico: Orale.

Peobody: Orale.

Chunky: Orale. Chicano Park really defined Chicanismo in a region that has never embraced it. On one side, you got conservative San Diego, and on the other side you got Tijuana, Mexico. And over there they never really liked us, they would call us Pocho, and Pocho is a derogatory term for Mexican-American, you know. But Pocho defines who and what we are, let's embrace our Pochismo man, fuck it I'm a Pocho! It's us. This park is us, this is sacred land.

Cósmico: Ho.

Peobody: Puro Red Steps, ese.

Chunky: Everything happens here ese, lowrider car shows, baptisms, Cinco de Mayo, wet T-shirt contests, danza. César Chávez came here many times. They're gonna build a sweat-lodge right over there. See that? Even the cops hang out here.

Peobody: Pinche pigs.

Cósmico: Hey man, we should go find Queso man, you guys gotta talk to Queso. Queso has the Master Plan, ese. You gotta talk to Queso.

Peobody: Yeah man. Find Queso.

Chunky: All this Queso talk is making me hungry ese. Let's go to Porkyland and get a quesadilla with no cheese, I'm still on my diet ese. C'mon vatos.

(They get ready to take off. Chunky stops, sees the mural, and looks right at the audience.)

Sabes que, don't ever underestimate the power and the beauty of Barrio Logan. This place went from junkyards to Chicano arte that is recognized all around the world and back again. Not bad for the little Mexican backyard of all this . . . opulence . . . San Diego. All the grandmothers and all the grandfathers, the elders that have gone before us, they watch over Chicano Parque at night like a protective spirit.

Cósmico: Ho.

Chunky: San Diego. Barrio Logan, puro Red Steps forever, homes. Hey Cósmico . . .

(Chunky accidently kicks over the paint can and steps on the mural.)

Cósmico: Hey, don't step on the mural, Chunky!
Chunky: Sorry, man.

(Chunky looks at the mural.)

Oh Cósmico, you've done a firme job on this mural ese, see right there people, he's got an Aztec sun right there next to the Black Magic Woman and the marijuana plant coming out of the maguey cactus, just like a Santana album cover. Chingao, it's beautiful, ese.

Peobody: Vida loca ese.
Chunky: How 'bout that poema now Cósmico?
Cósmico: Simón! I got it right here, vato.
Chunky: Hey, Peobody, can I sit on your bike?
Peobody: Chale.

(Cósmico pulls out a piece of brown paper and reads:)

Cósmico:

> Flying saucers in the air
> fly high like the huelga eagle
> above the Coronado
> soaring high high
> above Aztlán lan lan lan, lan lan lan
> recuerdos de mi pueblo
> mi San Diego that I love
> a San Diego for all gentes, all peoples
> brown, black, yellow, red and, yes, even white.

Peobody: Chale.

Cósmico:

> Simón.
> All of San Diego must come together one day.
> And that day will be soon.
> And that day will be . . .

(Cósmico flips paper over to the other side.)

And that day will be bigger than Cinco de Mayo!

Peobody: Chale.

Cósmico: Simón. Mi San Diego. I love you. Por Vida. Con Safos!

Chunky: Orale vato that was firme! A little trippy ese. You been watching the MeX-Files. You been smoking a lot of mota, huh? Come on vatos, let's go.

(They begin to exit but are stopped in their tracks by a harsh shaft of light from above. There are spaceship sounds like before. The sound and lights grow intense. A sucking sound is heard. The lights and sound change. Chunky disappears in the commotion.
Cósmico and Peobody are left alone on stage.)

Cósmico: Hey Peobody, what happened? Hey, where's Chunky?

Peobody: I don't know, ese. He disappeared or something.

(Cósmico looks up into the sky.)

Cósmico: Chingao, Chunky's been abducted by aliens!

Peobody: Orale.

Cósmico: Orale.

Peobody *(To audience)*: Can everyone say "orale"?

Audience: Orale.

(Blackout.)

Act 2

Secondary Inspection

Blackness. Sound of crickets. Someone whistles a signal. We hear the sound of a speeding truck come to a screeching stop. A door slams.

Mexican Militia Man: Alto! Alto!

(We hear panicked voices in English.)

Americans: Run! Run!

(People are running. The "truck lights" sweep the stage and the audience from left to right. A shotgun blast.
Lights up. Two Americans are caught, frozen like deer in harsh lights.
The Mexican Militia Man in cowboy hat and boots has captured the Americans on his property. The Americans in fatigues are frantic yet they fully comply. They are held at gun point by the Mexican Militia Man who holds an Uzi machine gun.
A coyote howls in the distance. We are deep in eastern Tijuana country.)

Mexican Militia Man: ¿Quiénes son cabrones? ¡Para abajo! ¿Qué hacen aquí?

(The Mexican Militia Man motions for the Americans to get down on the ground.)

American 1: Don't shoot, por favor. Soy actor, soy Chicano.

Mexican Militia Man: ¡Cállate puto! Qué Chicano y qué nada. ¿Eres D.E.A. verdad? Vas a morir. Horita.

(The Mexican Militia Man is about to shoot American 1.)

American 2: Please, sir, we're Americans! ¡Somos Americanos!

American 1: ¡Soy Chicano!

Mexican Militia Man: ¿Pochos?

American 1: ¡Sí! ¡Pochos!

American 2: Pocho power!

Mexican Militia Man: ¿Hablan Español?

American 1: ¡Sí, yo sabo poquito!

(The Mexican Militia Man searches their backpacks.)

Mexican Militia Man: ¿Tienen drogas? Do you have drugs?

American 1 and 2: No, sir.

Mexican Militia Man: Do you want drogas?

American 1: Uh . . . sure . . .

American 2: No!

(American 2 slaps American 1 upside the head.
The Mexican Militia Man rifles through their backpacks. He finds their theater schedule.)

Mexican Militia Man: ¿Qué es ésto? San Diego Repertory Theatre? ¡A sí, me gustó *Zoot Suit*! *(Strikes the classic Pachuco pose)*

American 1: Great, we're gonna get killed by a narco traficante who probably saw *Zoot Suit* nine times.

Mexican Militia Man: Ten times, cabrón! ¡Ándale cabrones! Get out of here!

American 1: C'mon, let's get the fuck out of here!

American 2 *(Taking out a tape recorder)*: Hey dude, why don't we interview him? ¿Señor, podemos entrevistarlo?

American 1: Sir, would you like to say something to the people of greater San Diego and Tijuana?

Mexican Militia Man: Sí como no.

(Speaking proudly into the tape recorder) ¡El Gobernador
Pete Wilson me puede besar el culo! Ha, ha, ha!
American 1: ¡Gracias, adiós!

*(We hear the same spaceship sounds from before. Lights pan across
the stage and audience.)*

Mexican Militia Man *(Looking up in amazement)*: ¡Qué chingadas!
¿Qué fue eso? Pinche gringos. Bueno me voy. ¡Qué viva
Mexico, cabrones! *(Exits into the night)*

(The Americans are dazed and a bit confused.)

American 2: That was a trip, dude.
American 1: Oh shit, he's coming back!

(The Mexican Militia Man, out of breath, darts back onstage.)

Mexican Militia Man: Excuse me, can you muchachos get me *Christmas Carol* tickets?
American 1: Sí . . .

(The Mexican Militia Man exits quickly. A coyote is heard.)

(Into tape recorder) Note to self, two front row *Christmas Carol*
tickets for Mr. and Mrs. Narco Traficante, they can sit right
next to Mr. and Mrs. Shit-kicker. *(Clicks off the tape recorder)*
This place is fucking weird.

*(Blackout. During this transition, we hear a radio montage of real
Tijuana radio stations. Two stagehands place a small cyclone
fence—"the border"—with small lights on it down center stage.
The stagehands lay large blanket-size flags on each side of the fence:
one flag is American, the other Mexican. The stagehands are setting
up a "bed." The stagehands exit.*
*The lights change as a Mexican Woman enters and prays on her
knees next to the "Mexican" side of the bed.*
*An American Man, the husband of the Mexican Woman, enters
and gets under the covers on his "U.S." side of the bed.*

The Mexican Woman makes the sign of the cross and goes under the covers on her side of the bed. Moments later, the American husband climbs over the "border" and makes love to his wife, roughly. She is indifferent but does not protest. After he is done with her, he climbs back over the fence to his side of the bed and covers himself with the American flag. He is fast asleep.

The Mexican Woman sits up and addresses the audience:)

Woman: The border is political. A symbol, an imposing monument impressed into our consciousness. It is that between fiction and nonfiction.

(To her husband) Husband!

Man: What is it, wife?

Woman: I love you. Do you love me?

(He does not answer. She lies back down and covers herself with her Mexican flag. The American Man sits up and addresses the audience:)

Man *(Almost in a whisper)*: I do love her and I need her, but I am embarrassed of her. I'm secretive. I take advantage of her. I cheat on her. Her Catholic upbringing seems to somehow allow my Protestant dark side to rear itself virtually unchecked.

(She sits up.)

Woman: I want to leave you! You're such an arrogant bastard. You are so thoughtless. Why are you so abusive?

Man: I am the best thing that's ever happened to you. You need me. Your children need me. And God knows how many you have!

Woman: What about your children? They come over to drink, to eat, to laugh, to soil. They get their fill and leave. They don't respect me!

Man: Honey, how can they respect you if you don't respect yourself?

(He lies down, turning his back on her once again.)

Woman *(To audience)*: There is a falsehood between us. I play the victim. When I'm with him I wear another face.

(She lies back down. He sits up.)

Man *(To audience)*: I don't trust her or her children. They want too much from me. I can't take my eyes off them for one second, her children of the serpent and eagle. Her children of the sun are sucking the tit of this country dry and I feel cheated by that, goddammit!

(The Man turns on the lights on top of the fence—the "border/bed" lights. They only light the Woman's side of the bed, and she gets upset by this.)

Woman: San Diego, why? Why do you do this to me?

Man: Because Tijuana you are mine and I love you too much. Now go to sleep.

(He turns the "border lights" to shine brightly on his wife. He lies down. She weeps. Then she crosses the fence to his side of the bed. She stands there.)

Woman: Our marriage is political. It is a physically imposing monument, a symbol impressed into our consciousness. Crucé el cerco. "I crossed the fence." This is a spiritual passage and a specific space of struggle and transgression. It is that between fiction and nonfiction.

(Augustin Lara's "Rival" is heard. The Mexican wife wakes up her American husband. He is startled at first. She asks him to dance. The husband rises to his feet and dances a slow and loving dance; they embrace like tango dancers, locked together, draped by their flag blankets. Lights slowly fade on them. The lovers exit.

A Mexican Intellectual enters to "process" the previous scene. He addresses the audience:)

Mexican Intellectual: Tijuana was created by the lust of San Diego. Everything that was illegal in your San Diego was permitted in her Tijuana. I have been observing this couple for years and, in fact, they have inspired my latest book: *Love in the Time of NAFTA,* subtitled *Americanos Asesinos,* available at Borders bookstores everywhere. Permit me to read: "Tijuana is not a backyard. It is here where Mexico starts, or is it here where America ends? Americans think they are entering a Hollywood version of a U.S. frontier town of a hundred years ago, with good guys and bad guys and wild women. ¡Qué estupidez! ¡Eso no es Tijuana! You see, here in Tijuana we have doctors, lawyers, teachers, universities, cultural centers, synagogues but, no, you would rather come here and take a picture, sitting on a zebra-painted donkey. ¡Qué absurdo!"

(An ominous Voice is heard offstage.)

Voice: Where are you from, buey?
Mexican Intellectual: I'm an educated expert from Mexico City. Soy Chilango.
Voice: Culero . . . Culero . . . Culero!

(The Mexican Intellectual exits in disgust. Taxi Driver Brujo, a strange character dressed as performance artist Guillermo Gómez-Peña, enters wearing rubber chickens, a black fedora and a punk-rock mariachi outfit.)

Taxi Driver Brujo: Good evening. Buenas noches. I am your cyber-transborder-virtual Tijuana taxi driver. Fasten your seat belts and have a shot of tequila.

Tijuana is an interactive CD-ROM in Español.
I did not swim across the border, I Riverdanced.
San Diego should change its name to North Tijuana.
An overpriced assimilated burrito is called a "wrap."
Angel hair pasta is fideo!
Next time you are at Taco Bell, order a quesadilla
    without cheese.
We didn't cross the border, the border crossed us.
Avenida Revolución is multiculturalism without a
    grant.

I have a striptease chihuahua that performs computer
laptop dancing. Ironic no?
Double-click your Border Brujo icon to exit this
transborder experience.
You are now cyber-wetbacks.
You are now cyber-wetbacks.
You are now cyber-wetbacks . . .

(Taxi Driver Brujo exits.
Lights reveal a young Mexican Worker, a maquiladora [factory]
worker. The mechanical hum of a busy Tijuana factory is always
heard. An offstage BBC Reporter translates into a microphone.)

Worker: La mayoridad de la gente que trabajan en la maquiladora son del campo y ochenta por ciento somos mujeres.

Reporter: The majority of the maquiladora [factory] workers are
from the fields and eighty percent are women.

Worker: Las maquiladoras trabajan las veinti-cuatro horas. Hay
tres turnos. Yo empiezo a las once de la noche y salgo a las
siete de la mañana. Tengo cuatro ninos y se quedan solos
toda la noche. Para no dormir en el trabajo, tomo café con
Coca-Cola, y a veces pastillas.

Reporter: The factories operate twenty-four hours and have three
shifts. Maria works from eleven P.M. till seven A.M. She has
four children whom she leaves alone all night. To stay alert
at work, she takes coffee mixed with Coca-Cola, and sometimes pills.

Worker: En la maqui no podemos hablar, reír, o masticar chicle.
Los baños no tienen puertas, nos dan solo un papelito, y
nos ponen el reloj.

Reporter: They are not permitted to talk, laugh or chew gum. The
lavatories are exposed to the factory and have no door. They
are timed with a stopwatch. The conditions are ghastly.

Worker: Yo trabajo para Mattel, y hacemos cosas que nunca
podría comprar. Los minivans para Barbie. Cuestan treinti-
cinco dólares en los Estados Unidos. Yo gano cuarenta
dólares a la semana.

Reporter: She works for Mattel Toy Manufacturers making acces-
sories for Barbie, things she could never afford in reality.

She also makes the toy minivans for Barbie, which in the States cost thirty-five American dollars. She earns forty American dollars a week. This is Nigel Miguel Lopez for the World News BBC, reporting from Tijuana, Mexico.

(A music and light transition. A dog barks ferociously. An American Ex-Marine appears with a cowboy hat, dog tags and Army-fatigue jacket. He drinks a Silver Bullet Coors beer.)

Ex-Marine *(To dog)*: Lady! Lady! You hush now. Lady, goddammit!

(The dog stops barking, the man takes a swig of beer and talks directly to the audience:)

What is it you guys wanna know? I'm a Vietnam vet, I'm a gringo, I been living in Tijuana for twenty years. There's a couple of guys from 'Nam that live here, enlisted fellas too, Army, Navy, Marines. They cannot afford to live in San Diego, so they live in TJ. And I don't think that's right, but I love it here. I love the people, the food, the culture—hell I married one of them.

(The Ex-Marine crouches down low as if he were at a campfire.)

I'll tell you what, when I first moved here this was nothing but dirt, and I don't own any of it, I'm just trying to make it better for the next feller to come along. Suppose that's the proper thing to do. I feel like I'm accepted here—never did feel like that in San Diego. I got good friends all throughout the colonia here . . .

(He waves to a neighbor in the audience.)

¡Buenas tardes, vecina! I tend not to look at people as Mexican or American, I try to look at each individual for the human goodness that they got right here—see? *(Gently taps his heart)*
    And I especially like to tell young people when I get my hands on 'em, I like to tell young people to just forget about

color, you know, just forget about what color somebody is. My god, America is so obsessed with what color you are and what your background is, just forget about color, just put it out of your head for one minute. Hell, I'm trying to forget about color right now that's how come I'm drinking so much today.

(He takes a swig of beer.)

Now if you look on down the street there, I know that might seem queer to some of you, but what we got down the street is two girl dogs humping on each other. Now they don't care if one dog is a gringo dog or if one's a Mexican dog, or if one's a girl dog or a boy dog—they're just humping on each other. They don't know right from wrong and I feel that we as human beings need to be a little bit more like them doggies down the street!

See, you can have real good people and you can have people that are real bad. Bad people don't like good people 'cause they're too good, and good people don't like bad people 'cause they're too bad and say, "I cannot accept you." But that's not what it's all about folks—shoot no—you see somebody hurting somebody else you ought to step in there and say, "Hey, you come deal with me."

Once a Marine always a Marine. The Corps don't teach you to go out and kill someone, no sir. The Corps teaches you to be aware. See, I'm gonna look left, I'm gonna look right, I'm gonna look up, I'm gonna look down, if I see somebody down I'm gonna say, "Hey, I can be there for ya."

The problem I see in America is that there's just too much violence up there—from the border up to Pendleton. I mean everybody's armed to the teeth, even little Junior next door—why he's got a semi-automatic aimed right at your head and some pipe bombs for your mailbox that he learned how to make on his computer thingy there. I'm afraid of that, yes sir. And now you got everybody waving their little flags and crying out for war. I've seen war, I've seen boys ripped limb to limb, I too have walked in the Valley of Death . . . *(Pause)* My god, it's not like a movie, folks, no sir. What I see happening in America, why it's not the country that I fought and nearly died for—it rips my heart out but I will not live in America.

Who was it that said patriotism is the last refuge to which a scoundrel clings? Check that out.

And if we could just forget about color for one goddamned minute there would be nothing, I mean nothing, that we could not achieve of as the human race.

(He points to his temple and then to the two girl dogs down the street.)

Them doggies down the street. Does anybody here know or care as to what I'm talking about?

(The Ex-Marine walks off.
A music and light transition. The following four characters are played by two actors. One actor plays Donna and Paolo, the other actor plays Amy and Oscar.)

Donna: This used to be a white middle-class neighborhood, now it's got everybody. It used to be called East San Diego. Now it's called City Heights. It's like they decided to put all the poor people of all races all in one place, so you won't have to deal with them anywhere else.

Amy: That's right.

Donna: I moved here about ten years ago. Just right after you did, right, Amy?

Amy: Yeah.

Donna: And then all these foreigners started moving in . . .

Amy: They're Americans, Donna, they're new Americans.

Paolo: Hello. Congratulations to you.

Oscar: Thank you. Ah, congratulations to you. New Americans.

Paolo: Yes, new Americans. Pretty soon. My name is Paolo.

Oscar: My name is Oscar.

Paolo: Oh, you drive taxi?

Oscar: No, those are the Ethiopians. Let me guess, you are from Philippines and you live in Mira Mesa?

Paolo: Yes, yes. Manila Mesa as they call it.

(They laugh.)

Did you know San Diego has the highest Filipino population in the world after Manila? And it's because of the Navy. We were recruited to serve, and once we got established here we brought our families over.

Oscar: Coming from Africa to the U.S. is like night and day, I am telling you. For example, talking about time in my country, a meeting like today will begin when you get there. *(Laughter)* Paolo, tell me something, why is it that the Filipino is so loyal to United States?

Paolo: We feel a kind of loyalty to the United States, because we fought side by side with them against our enemies. We say "Utangaloob." "Utan" means a debt, "loob" means inside. So a debt that you feel, inside, towards someone that has done you a favor. A favor you will never be able to repay in a lifetime.

Amy: When I first got here I was pretty fearless. Robert, my husband, and I were getting out of a community meeting, and I wanted to get a pack of cigarettes on University Avenue. I got my purse on my shoulder, we're walking down the alley and we saw a guy standing there and I knew something was wrong, it didn't look right, you know?

Donna: That's because you're a city dog, Amy. You sense these things.

Amy: Yeah, yeah, so I put my purse on the other side and keep walking. Suddenly the guy steps in front of us! And I'm standing there going, "I can't believe I'm being mugged." He's got his hand in his coat, I guess he's holding a gun. And I'm thinking, Robert, my husband, is going to get blown away over a pack of cigarettes.

Donna: It's those foreigners, Amy . . .

Amy: New Americans, Donna.

Donna: . . . they call all their relatives, move into one small house. You got Vietnamese kids running all over the alley back there. Every Saturday night the Mexicans over there play their loud music!

Amy: It's called "quebradita" music, "quebradita."

Donna: It sounds all the same to me! I remember catching a little African boy scribbling on the wall back there. I told him you better stop or else you're going to grow up to be a nigger.

Amy: Oh god, please Donna! Don't use that word. Oh god.

Donna: Any civil war that erupts, they send their refugees over here. I suppose the Afghanistans are coming next.

Paolo: Oscar, do you know the bamboo? The bamboo is a very tall plant that blows with the wind. Wherever the wind blows, the bamboo does not resist it, it goes with it. Filipinos are like the bamboo. We assimilate just like the bamboo.

Oscar: You know, Paolo, I escaped from Uganda. I escaped basically because of government persecution. I am telling you. There's a lot of things here I am not used to. Freedom. Especially freedom.

Amy: After the guy mugged us, I ran to the Chinese BBQ. I was absolutely hysterical. So I'm banging and screaming on their screen door, yelling, "Open up, they're after me, they're gonna kill me, let me in." And there's these four Chinese guys, or Vietnamese, I don't know . . .

Donna: New Americans, Amy.

Amy: Yeah, they're just sitting there smiling at me! So we ran to the back of another restaurant. And they have this big African-American guard and I ask him, "Did you see anything?" And he said, "No I didn't see anything." And I know he saw something.

Donna: Of course he saw it. He just doesn't give a shit!

Oscar: I love City Heights, I am telling you. It's like the United Nations. My neighbors are Somalians, Guatemalans, Laotians, Nigerians, Lebanese, Russians . . .

Paolo: Filipinos?

Oscar: Yes, Filipinos too.

Paolo: Pinoy power!

Oscar: You know, Paolo, I believe we all come here because the weather here reminds us of home.

Paolo: Yes, home.

Oscar: Home. *(Beat)* Paolo, do you think we will ever go back home?

Paolo: Oscar, we are home.

(A Pakistani-American with a turban, mustache and suit enters.)

Pakistani-American: Everyone rise, raise your left hand, and repeat after me.

Paolo and Oscar: I pledge allegiance to the flag of the United States of America, and to the Republic for which it stands, one nation under God, indivisible, with liberty and justice for all.

Pakistani-American: Congratulations, gentlemen. You are new Americans!

("America the Beautiful" is heard. The men wave little American flags with pride and hope. Lights fade out.

Techno house-music with deep bass is heard. An Asian Car Gang Guy in baggy Tribal Gear hip-hop clothes enters. His movements are b-boy precise and in rhythm to the beats. The music stops abruptly.)

Asian Car Gang Guy: All my friend are Hmong, Laotian, Vietnamese, Cambodian, Korean, Hapa, Chinese. We an all-

Asian car crew and party crew here in San Diego. Hold on, my pager blowin' up like motherfuckuh.

(He checks his lime green pager.)

Ah, Asian booty call, for real foo. It's my girlfriend, Miso. Miso horny!

My car crew there no white people, no Mexican people, no black, just Asian. We like to drive only the Acura, Prelude, Accord . . . man, other pager blowin' up like motherfuckuh . . .

(He checks his purple pager.)

Damn, I popular today. I wanted to tell you my best friend in the whole world his name is Winston. He my dog, my backup, my homeboy, he my niggah—oh no we not prejudice, he not black or nothing, that's just the way we talk foo: "Wassup niggah, wassup niggah." His grandmother called yesterday from Ho Chi Minh City, she call and she say, "A que quan ho pho." Do you know what that mean? "Wassup niggah," for real foo.

The other day, we race Mexican crew in National City, by the border where all the Mexicans live, ooh, it's nasty over there, foo. We race, my car here, Mexican guy car right there. Green light go, my car beat Mexican guy car so bad yo! I was like, "Wassup Mexican?" And they got mad at me and surround me and my car and they say, "Wassup Chinaman?" I thought they gonna kill me for sure. Then my dog Winston, I didn't know, he had a .45 under his car seat, he put the .45 right to Mexican guy head . . .

(Asian Car Gang Guy puts his hand to his head like a pistol.)

. . . and he say, "I gonna kill you Mexican, I blow your brain out right now." I was like damn yo, that was scandalous. We got the hell outta there, we go back to Circle K on El Cajon where we belong. And when we got there Winston grab me outta my Acura and he throw me up

against the wall and I say, "Wassup homeboy wassup?" He say, "No wassup, you made me almost kill Mexican guy for nothing. Of course you beat him, he drive lowrider, he go low and slow!" I have to say wassup to myself.

Shit, third pager blowin' up like motherfuckah.

(Asian Car Gang Guy checks his red pager.)

Ah damn, it's grandfather, for real, foo. Grandfather say, "Wassup niggah?"

(Blackout. Lights up on a lesbian couple, Jennifer and Tilly, holding Starbucks coffee cups.)

Jennifer and Tilly: Warm soy milk!
Jennifer: Oh, hi! We're really happy you're interviewing us. I'm Jennifer and this is Tilly.
Tilly: Hi.
Jennifer: We live in the suburbs, which is Carmel Mountain Ranch, which is between Poway and Rancho Bernardo. There's a lot of old people that live there, but recently a lot

of young people have been moving in, so I gave our neighborhood a new motto and the motto is: "Newlywed or Nearly Dead."

Tilly: It's a cool neighborhood. It's the kind where you drive up to your driveway, open your automatic garage door, drive in, close the door. So you really never get to know your neighbors. Just recently the straight parents began waving hello to us. But still they're really protective with their kids.

Jennifer: Especially during Halloween. We set everything up, got the candy, got the skeleton for the door, we were all dressed up, dressed up even our dog. We were so stoked. But no one came to our door, not one kid.

Tilly: We were so bummed that finally I went outside and knocked on our own door. Jennifer opened it up and gave me the candy.

Jennifer: As a lesbian I have never felt discrimination as much because it's not something I walk into. So I don't see a lot of it.

Tilly: But it gets pretty annoying sometimes. Guess what happened the other day? This guy comes up and asks me, "So you don't care for the salami?"

Jennifer: What a fucking man pig.

Tilly: And I said to him, "No thank you, I'm a vagi-tarian!"

(They both laugh and slap each other five.
Surfer ska music crashes in. Three surfer dudes, Todd, Tad and Troy, mosh and fool around like stoners. The music fades.)

Todd: Ha, ha, ha, um, um, I was like just remembering that time the waves got so big. You guys remember the Scripps Observation Tower, the one out in the channel? Remember when the wave came right over the tower and just knocked it right in the water? It was like whoa . . . The tower just crashed. My best friend Troy, you guys remember Troy don't you?

Tad: Oh yeah . . .

Todd: My friend Troy was standing over there on the jetty where like the boats go out to like the ocean and stuff like that, he was standing there dude and the wave came right over ol' Troy. You know what he did? He jumped on his board and he started surfing the wave in reverse from the beach back to the ocean! The wave was so humongous, it was breaking in reverse from Mission Boulevard back to the water and I don't even know if you people know what I'm fuckin' talkin' about 'cause I barely do. It was a gnarly wave man, what year was that dudes?

Troy: Oh, that was like '85.

Tad: Nah, that was like '82, man.

Troy: Nah, '85

Todd: It was '89, dudes.

(After a beat, they share a wicked laugh.)

Tad: We don't fuckin' remember!

Todd: We don't remember, 'cause we're stoners!

Troy: El Niño's been good for us. Earthquakes, tidal waves—it could be Armageddon, the end of the world and the boys will still be surfing. Nonstop.

Todd: No doubt, no doubt, no doubt.

Tad: Hey guys, talk about the end of the world, I was macking with some chick on the beach last night . . .

Todd: Sweet.

Tad: Oh yeah . . . and I saw a UFO.

Troy: No way, Tad.

Tad: I swear to fuckin' God, I saw a UFO. I wasn't even smoking, OK?

Todd: What's up with you swearing like that Tad? Using God's name like that, dude. What's wrong with you, dude? There's a bunch a kids out here on the beach, their parents are gonna get fuckin' pissed off dude and God's gonna punish you and make you wipe out on a wave and it's gonna hurt really bad like that time we had to kick the shit outta you!

(The surfers mock-fight with each other.)

Troy: Tittie twister!

Todd: Last year we didn't know who this doofus was.

Troy: Yea, he was a barney from Santa Cruz.

Todd: You can't just come surfing in other peoples' water Tad, you gotta respect the borders and the boundries even in the ocean. Whenever I surf I.B., O.B. or P.B., I have total respecto, because if the boys see strange faces in the water, they'll go loco on you and start whomping on you and it could hurt really really bad.

Tad: Talk about strange faces, have you seen Kevin's sister lately?

Todd: Sweet.

Tad: No, dude. She got really gnarly looking.

Troy: No way, dude, she was a hot tamale in high school.

Tad: Oh yeah, but now, she's like a dog, it's really sad.

(After a very long beat, they bust up laughing. Another beat.)

Todd: So what ya dudes wanna do now?

(We hear a wave crashing, the surfer dudes move slightly upstage and back again so they don't get wet from the water.)

Whoa . . .

(We hear another wave crashing. The surfer dudes move upstage and laugh wickedly.
Lights change. We hear a Patient talking to a psychiatric Doctor.)

Patient: Well, Doc, I'm a little embarrassed, quite frankly. Where do I begin? I'm just tired of being the poster boy for this city.

Doctor: Why don't you just sit back, relax, and talk about whatever comes to your mind. Take your time.

Patient: My shrink says take my time. Hah!

(Lights come up. Lying on a chaise longue is Shamu the killer whale from Sea World. He sounds like a whiny Woody Allen.)

Shamu: Day after day, people don't know what it's like to perform stupid tricks, make big splashes, kiss the kiddies! Yesterday, Doc, I literally tried to bite the hand that feeds me!

Doctor: How did that make you feel?

Shamu: It felt great. Natural-like. Second nature, you know. Made me really miss my mother.

Doctor: How do you feel towards your mother?

Shamu: I love my mother, it's my dad I can't stand. He runs off with some shiksa two days before I was born! I hope he ends up in a fucking tuna can!

Doctor: Okay Shammy, I'm going to ask you, what's really bothering you?

Shamu: Dolphin-free Chicanos.

Doctor: I don't understand?

Shamu: The other day, in between shows, me and some of the other mammals are swimming around, shooting the breeze blowing off some salt water, coming down from the show buzz, you know?

Doctor: Sure. Go on.

Shamu: Well, I can hear the trainers yapping away about how I was bringing down the rest of the team with my negative attitude. Then I couldn't believe what my sonar was picking up, the director of the park wants to bring in some Mexican killer whales to do the shows. Now these whales have no documentation, no work permits, no papers, no real training, but they work for cheap and eat less fish. It's a fucking crime, Doc! I mean I am not a racist killer whale, I just want some job security and time off with less shows. Did you know Free Willy was a Guatemalan? His real name is Guillermo!

Doctor: Very interesting.

Shamu: Am I being unreasonable here? I mean, I wouldn't go to Ensenada and take their jobs away. I'd probably end up a fish taco!

Doctor: Take it easy, Shammy.

Shamu: "Take it easy, Shammy"? Take it easy? You take it easy! I'm talking about Mexican whales here, Doc. Mexican fuckin' whales! My god! Killer fuckin' wetback whales are coming! Eeeeeiiii . . .

(The agitated Shamu charges the Doctor.)

Doctor: Take a fish, Shammy! Take a fish!

(Blackout.
  Lush, meloncholy jazz is heard. The stage is awash in blue
light. Richard, a poet, enters.)

Richard: Gilbert Castellano's trumpet blows like a gentle wind
under the Coronado Bridge, through the Logan, down to
Chula Vista y San Ysidro, Imperial Beach, and swirls up La
Costa to Oceanside and then takes the Poway Highway to
Jennie's house.

The wind stirs up the ghosts and the chicken shacks near
Lemon Grove, where Archie Moore could get a free meal
and a cold beer before he became champ of the world—rest
in peace.

I can see Grandmother Moon now rising low and lazy
off the Palomar Mountains to the east. I can see it hanging
over the military factory of melancholy, the Balboa Naval
Hospital where I was born. (The moon always changes
color when you go to Mexico.)

And hobo spirits take the night train to Old Town.
Fishing used to be good on Mission Bay. And mobster
ghosts roll dice in the back room of the El Cortez. Sam
Rothstein and those retired, Vegas mobsters in La Jolla
never met La Eme. (La Eme says no more drive-by's in the
barrio. I thought they said "drive-throughs." I haven't had a
Happy Meal since 1989.)

And tonight the vatos are fighting the Negroes under the
bridge because last night's dance changed everything that
tragic summer of '47, when Chaleco got killed!

And Pachuco old-timers will tell you of their favorite
Jewish tailor on Market Street. Expert ducktails from black
barbers on Broadway. I hear Chon got blew up in Korea
with his cousin from Lomas. Who's gonna tell Comadre?

Spring time in San Diego and places like Little Jack's
Corner, Yucca Flats, Cherry Nob Hill, Golden Hill,
Mockingbird Hill, look out! And white port and lemon

juice shake-'em-ups in those times of the atomic bomb. And San Diego's racist cops when Consolidated was camouflaged on the PCH.

The Lemon Grove incident generation has now
    reached their eighties.
Wolfman Jack and the mighty six-ninety.
Tom Metzger still wears a purple hooded nighty.
You sexy Fallbrook motherfucker.
Balboa stadium, 1963 Louis Rey, black sprinter
Don Bajema, the fastest white boy in San Diego
jump those hurdles
jump that fence
in reverse
to
Chicles and the Gertrude Stein of Tijuana
where we find a TJ we did not know existed
were we find a version of ourselves
in the land of the oblique
we find Paris in TJ
and we find something shameful
I am the ugly American who averts eye contact
with Indian beggars in the street on my way to Baby
    Rock.
Brushing up against new Tijuana money, powerful
    Juniors, 18th Street pelones,
Norte/Sur, Special Forces, cross-dressers and
    Chiapas refugees.
How many Mayans in the mosh pit?
A Mexican is not a Mexican is not a Mexican.

It's three A.M. in Tijuana and I am with a prostitute as banda music plays from the sidewalk below. It's three A.M. in Tijuana and I am the prostitute and banda music plays from the sidewalk below.

Border officer to motorist: "What are you bringing back into the country, sir?" Answer: "Just a lowered sense of self-esteem."

Secondary inspection, secondary inspection . . .

I am in a foreign country now—San Diego. Where we find Chicano surfers in Imperial Beach with WHITE POWER tattooed on their forearms and white boys in Sherman with TRES OCHO tattooed across their stomachs.

Nothing is what it appears to be here.

Everytime I'm in San Diego, Spellcheck on my computer changes the word "Chicano" to "Chicanery."

And no longer will my paradigm of paradise parallel the paradox that walks the streets of Tijuana or San Diego or the reservation or the penitentiary at the three A.M.

Normal Heights, abnormal lows.

And tonight I'm just a gas-lamp loser.

But you know something? On the night that I was born, my mom tells me, from her hospital room at Balboa Naval, across from the San Diego Zoo, she could hear the lions roar.

(Lights slowly fade out.

We hear foghorns. We are under the Coronado Bridge, we hear the traffic above. It is three A.M., the Clashers are looking for the legendary Queso of Barrio Logan.)

Richard *(Sotto voce)*: Queso? Queso? Hello, I'm looking for Queso.
Ric: Queso?

(Behind the shadows emerges a man who appears to be ten feet tall. Dashing, gray-haired and dressed in a long, black trench coat and white silk scarf.)

Queso: I am Queso? What can I do for you young men?
Richard: We were told to meet you here, under the bridge.
Queso: Yes?
Ric: We understand you have a plan, or "the plan"?
Queso: Shhh. Come closer. I don't want to wake up my neighbors.
Richard: What is your plan about?
Queso: The plan? That is something I want to share with the whole world.

Ric: That's great, because to tell you the truth, this place is driving us a little crazy. We can't seem to figure it out.

Queso: Buried deep in the bay, at the very depths of our soul are pylons that hold up the majestic Coronado Bridge. Those pylons have been driven deep into Mother Earth. It is there where you may find the soul, secrets and corazón, the very hearts of San Diego and Tijuana.

Richard: So "the plan" is about the bridge?

Queso: It's about the light, the solstice, the geological and ecological understandings of that ortho-tropic bridge structure!

Ric: So it's the physical structure? I'm sorry, I'm lost.

Queso: Mijos, you must understand what lives and what dies in the San Diego Bay. The Indians knew this. I have studied the murky filth and the Peregrine Falcons that nest on the bridge. And the seagulls—seagulls everywhere, screaming and screeching—send me back to my childhood when I swam in the bay with the neighborhood kids as the guano plant, the sewage plant and the 32nd Naval dumped poisons in the bay, our home. The smell was putrid! The stench from rotting carcasses from the Tuna and Albacore canneries where our parents worked their hands and fingers to the bone.

Richard: That's beautiful, Queso, but explain to us, about the bridge.

Queso: It's not just a bridge! It's a great symphonic movement of paint, sculpture and people! Let the bridge symbolize the bridging of all our communities. Let it bridge the past with the present. Where there is no beginning or end. Our higher self.

Richard: And the Peregrine Falcons . . . I'm trying to write all this down.

Queso: Your imagination is flaring. Don't write now, just listen. You must go deep—deep as the very bay itself. You must go back, you must go back before you can go forward—look over there.

Ric: I don't see anything.

(We see a ghostly image of an Indian, mid-dance in ceremony. We hear haunting and beautiful Native music.)

Queso: Go back, dig deeper and deeper, listen to the elders. They will tell you what you desperately need to know.

Richard: You mean like how to end this play?

Queso: Oh, it never ends. It's infinite. Keep it simple!

(Queso starts to do a Native American chant.)

Richard: What are you doing?

Queso: Communicating! . . .

(The intense sound of a spaceship and lights fill the stage. It reaches a climax and then silence. Ric and Richard are now alone.)

Richard: Where did he go?

Ric *(Calling out)*: Queso? Queso?

Richard: He vanished.

Ric: Let's get out of here. This place is kind of spooky.

Richard: This place is fucking weird.

Ric: Where did we leave the car?

Richard: Avocado level.

Ric: No, onion.

Richard: I think it was asparagus.

Ric: Are you sure it wasn't tomato? . . .

(The Clashers exit. Cosmic space sounds are heard. The Bald Man with the purple gown and Nike sneakers from earlier in the play appears center stage.)

Bald Man: The New millennium marked the close of a major cycle and will initiate a spiritual renaissance of logic and reason. The end of the millennium is also the end of the Dark Ages, what the Aztecs call "El Quinto Sol." As we enter this new era, we must leave behind the negative feelings of our lower self. The hatred, the fear, the unresolved conflicts. Our ancestors know of a place, a place where there are no borders, only infinitesimal possibilities . . .

(The two Clashers return. Space music builds. The Clashers join hands with the Bald Man and face the audience. Gradually they

form a tableau of a freeway crossing sign that warns of Illegal Aliens crossing the highway.

We hear the Beach Boys' "Good Vibrations." Lights and sound slowly fade to black.)

The End

Nuyorican Stories

NEW YORK CITY

ACKNOWLEDGMENTS

Culture Clash thanks the families of Miguel Piñero and Ricardo Sánchez for the usage of their poetry. Additional thanks to "El Reverendo" Pedro Pietri and Miguel Algarín. This piece would have been impossible without the love and support of Olgui Robles-Toro, Máximo Colón, Frank Algarín, María Irene Fornes, Tito Lespier, Cristina Verán, David Wallace, Betty and Constance Rodgers, Iris Morales, Crazy Leggs, Danny Hoch, Felipe Luciano, the family of Lucky CienFuegos, Sarah Jones, Roger Guenveur Smith, the family of Héctor Lavoe, Brooks Loro, Omar Ramírez, Mario Ruiz and Michelle Carlo.

Introduction to NUYORICAN STORIES

By Herbert Siguenza

Nuyorican Stories was commissioned by INTAR through a grant by the National Theatre Residency Program. We spent six months in New York City living, dying, drinking and wandering around the big concrete island. We really didn't know what our piece about New York City was going to be about. Where does one start in such a big city full of stories? Besides, it was difficult sitting a New Yorker down for an interview. They just don't like to talk to strangers from California, you know? We were lost and we needed a breakthrough.

Our breakthrough, our inspiration, was sparked by another artist and scholar, Miguel Algarín, founding member of the legendary Nuyorican Poet's Café. Along with poets Pedro Pietri, Lucky CienFuegos and Felipe Luciano, Algarín and the Café sparked the Nuyorican Poets Movement. We spent a wonderful afternoon with Miguel in his apartment on the Lower East Side or "Loisaida" as the residents call it. Our piece is built around the rich stories he told us that day and the pride he felt showing us his barrio and introducing us to his gente. I remember he took us to a mom-and-pop restaurant and we had an unforgettable feast of pollo fricassee, arroz con gandules, tostones and the garlicky mofongo. ¡Vaya!

Back in his apartment, Miguel recounted his early days of the Café and the road trips he took to California in the 1970s to exchange poetry with West Coast Chicano poets. Some of these Chicano poets made trips back east including Richard Montoya's father José, the late Ricardo Sánchez and Culture Clash member, José Antonio Burciaga. Aha! We finally found the thesis of our play—the cultural, political and spiritual connection between Chicanos and Nuyoricans. Two marginalized communities with a strong sense of culture, community and defiance. Inspired by the Black Panther Movement of self-empowerment and liberation, in the early 1970s the Chicano and Nuyorican Movements almost simultaneously created their own political organizations such as the La Raza Unida Party and the Young Lords Party.

We had the honor of sitting down with two very strong women: Olguie Robles-Toro and filmmaker Iris Morales (*¡Palante, Siempre Palante! The Young Lords*) who were members of the Lords and are still very active in the community. They told us of their personal sacrifice of being part of the Movement but also the gains it has had on social services and education. We also interviewed Máximo Colón, a pro-Independent Puerto Rico supporter and photographer, who gave us his views about the "state of limbo" his island-nation has endured since the U.S. colonization one hundred years ago.

Even though the 1970s were a restless and agitated political time, you cannot talk about the era without discussing its music and fashion. The explosion of salsa music was an important cultural and social element for Puerto Ricans dancing to the "New York salsa sound" at clubs such as Corso's. A sound that influenced West Coast Chicano artists, such as Carlos Santana, Malo and El Chicano. The music of Willie Colón and the haunting voice of the late Héctor Lavoe is definitely the soundtrack to that polyester era.

The energy of the Lower East Side and the Nuyorican Poets Movement was instrumental to the birth of hip-hop culture (rap, break-dancing, graffiti art, deejay-ing) and even modern-day spoken-word slams. Unfortunately, the era was also one of drug abuse that clouded the Movement. Maverick poet and playwright Miguel Piñero was one of many casualties. For Piñero "Mi Vida Loca" was not just a slogan, but a way of living life to the fullest. His poetry and spirit is the tying thread of the piece. Adios Miguelito, adios.

PRODUCTION HISTORY

Nuyorican Stories premiered at INTAR Hispanic American Arts Center (Max Ferrá, Artistic Director) in New York City on September 22, 1999. The director was Max Ferrá; the set design was by Van Santvoord, the lighting design was by Phillip D. Widmer, the costume design was by Donna Zakowska, the sound design was by Johnna Doty; the production manager was Richard Callahan, the visual consultant was Juan Sánchez and the stage manager was B. D. White.

A dark stage. Santana's "Samba Pa Ti" is heard. The house lights slowly come down. Total darkness. Then a "street corner" light comes up. Richard enters.

Richard: Sometime in 1974, a Nuyorican poet and playwright, named Miguel Piñero, was standing on a corner somewhere on the Lower East Side with several Chicano poets from the West Coast. One of those poets was my father José Montoya, another was José Antonio Burciaga, one of the founding members of our group . . .

(Ric and Herbert enter.)

Ric and Herbert: Rest in peace.

Richard: Rest in peace, brothers. They were drinking, jiving and getting very high, when suddenly Piñero turned serious and posed a question to the poets gathered there on that corner. The question was this: "What is the greatest Chicano poem ever written?" They thought about it. No one said anything. Then, Piñero lifted up his shirt sleeve and there tattooed on his arm, were three words . . . "Mi Vida Loca."

Ric and Herbert: Mi Vida Loca.

Richard: My crazy life. That, Piñero said, was the greatest Chicano poem ever written. Then our literary gods stumbled into a van and headed to the Bronx with cops chasing them.

*(Police sirens are heard in the distance. Santana's "Oye Como Va"
is heard.)*

Bajando . . . Bajando . . .
Ric: Bajando . . .
Herbert: Bajando . . . Bajando . . .
Richard: We have to find Lucky . . .
Ric: Looking for Lucky . . . Nueva Yol, baby.
Herbert: Lucky, make me lucky . . . viva Puerto Rico libre!

(Music transition into El Chicano's "Viva Tirado.")

Richard:

> In the beginning God created the ghettos and the slums
> and God saw that this was good
> so God said let there be more ghettos and more slums
> But God saw that this was plain
> So to decorate, God created lead-base paint!

Ric:

> From the island of Puerto Rico
> To the isle of Manhattan
> Soy Taino de mi bello Boriquen
> Called "The Land of the Brave Lord."
> The Arawak Indians
> Blood brothers of my past
> Aquí les toco mi tambor!

Herbert:

> On the third day
> because on the second day God was out of town,
> On the third day
> God's nose was runnin' and his jones was comin' down
> and God in his all-knowing wisdom, knew he needed
>   a fix!

Ric:

> The blood that runs through me is
> Spanish, Indian and African

sixteenth-century chants de
Jíbaros slaving side by side
Taínos y Africanos
Cultivating the fertile soil
Sugar cane, tobacco, spices,
And playing the first game of dominoes!

Ric and Richard: Vaya!

Herbert:

And with this marriage aquí les va
Trigueños, blancos, Indios
Yoruba spirits—black sky
Negros sigh, el coquí canta y
Las Indias cooking
Sofrito en esta isla del encanto!

Richard:

On the fourth day God was riding around Harlem
    in a gypsy cab when he created the people, don't
    you know
but he saw the people lonely and hungry
and from his eminence rectum
he created a companion for these people
and he called this companion

All: Capitalism!
Richard: The "Genesis" according to Miguelito Piñero.
Ric and Herbert: Word!

Richard:

And when Ponce de León looked upon the shores and
shouted . . .

Herbert: "¡Vale vale, qué Puerto Rico!"

Richard:

And so when the first Puerto Rican
Landed upon the shores of New York City he shouted . . .

Ric: "Damn it's cold, bro!"

(Willie Colón's "Murga" blasts in. The actors strike poses, like snapshots after each music stab:
1. *Fists in the air*
2. *Street fighting*
3. *Pointing guns at each other*
4. *Police pointing gun at suspect on ground*
5. *Shooting up heroin*
6. *Police frisking a suspect*
7. *Sodomizing*
8. *See no evil, speak no evil, hear no evil.*
Police sirens are heard again. All the actors dance salsa. Richard and Herbert leave dancing. Ric continues to dance and puts on a cap with the Puerto Rican flag sewn on it. The music stops. He freezes on a fire escape ladder. Blackout.

Lights crossfade to street scene. Nuyorican poet and professor, Miguel Algarín enters followed by Herbert as himself.)

Miguel *(On cell phone)*: Isabel! It's me Miguel. It's so funny that you called, so I'm calling you back. *(To Herbert)* Isabel is a professor at Rutgers. *(Back on cell phone)* I have here with me a Chicano gentleman from the Coast. What's your name again? . . .

Herbert: Herbert.

Miguel: His name is Herbert. He's with Culture Clash, the theater group. They are interviewing people who were living and working in Loisaida in the mid to late '70s. Do you remember, girl? Ha, ha. No, I'm on this young man's cell phone, he was nice enough to let me use it, you see. No, I'm leaving tomorrow to Austin, then I come back Sunday. Then I go to Colombia on Monday. They're going to give me an award or something. You know, for my contribution to poetry and culture . . . Yes, for my book, *Love Is Hard Work.* Yes, I'm teaching a course on Shakespeare at NYU, but for two weeks I go to London, from the nineteenth on . . . Is that when you want me to do the Neruda poem? Oh, the festival has been canceled . . . I see. You want me to get Toni Morrison? I can call Amiri Baraka if you like? Well, it

just so happens I'm seeing Toni tomorrow . . . Hallo? Hallo? *(To Herbert)* I lost her, we got cut off or something . . .

(Miguel starts to slam the cell phone against his leg.)

Herbert: No, no. Please don't do that . . .

(Miguel gives Herbert his cell phone back, then stops to talk to someone across the street.)

Miguel: Hola, Adela, cómo está baby? Will you be open today, mi negrita? We'll be over for lunch, this is uh . . . what's your name again?
Herbert: Herbert.
Miguel: Yes, of course. Where were we?
Herbert: 1974.
Miguel: Yes, in 1974 we really began to feel our importance as artists and poets here in New York City. Miguel Piñero's *Short Eyes* was on Broadway and we had just opened the Nuyorican Poet's Café down here in Loisaida.

Herbert: Is that when you met Richard's father?

Miguel: Who's his father?

Herbert: The Chicano poet José Montoya.

Miguel: José! Yes! I know him well. He's with the Royal Chicano Air Force.

Herbert: They fly adobe airplanes.

Miguel: Marijuaneros! Locos . . . Ha . . . ha . . . ha. Oh yeah, they were a very important influence on the Coast. You see, the Chicanos were having their big "Great Society" bashes when Lucky CienFuegos, Mickey and I got into my Dodge van and drove out west to Texas. We would arrive with poetry that y'all didn't even begin to think was possible! When we got to Texas, the Chicanos were saying: "The Nuyoricans are coming! The Nuyoricans are coming!" And when we got out of the van in Corpus Christi, people went: "Fuck!" Lucky CienFuegos came out of the van stepping off with these huge platform shoes because he was a small guy, but he had a tremendous, developed, cut torso. He had these long bell-bottoms to cover up his skinny-ass legs and these short vests. And then this huge afro! Papi. My van was called the "Fuck You Van."

Herbert: The "Fuck You Van"?

Miguel: Yeah. One night, Mickey, Lucky and I were getting busy with these three Chicanas in the van. And then we would say: "Switch!" And then we would jump rabbit-style over each other and fuck the other one! Ha, ha, ha! Those three Chicanas, I am quite sure they have Ph.Ds by now. Yeah, I know all about you guys. You Chicanos. Your intellectuals are full of shit! They're all sold-out and corrupted, and they still are. Our intellectuals are full of shit, too! But our intellectuals lived close to us. They had to answer directly to us. It's not as big as Texas or California. We live close to each other so your ass is in trouble if you write an essay saying some shit that don't mean nothing. Our intellectuals had to be more honest. But not much more. But your intellectuals hid in academia. I know all about you guys. You guys would argue all the time. Get drunker and drunker and meaner and meaner. Tigre fist fighting with Ricardo Sánchez, someone had a gun. Lorna Dee Cervantes and other Chicana sisters trying to be heard. And I remember Richard's father José getting very mad because all the Chicanos would fuck with each other's ego and tear down what they were trying so hard to build. Meanwhile, us Nuyoricans, we was drinking your wine, smoking your weed and fucking your women! Ha, ha, ha!

(Herbert's cell phone rings.)

Herbert: Hello? Yes, one moment. It's for you, Algarín.

(Herbert gives Miguel his cell phone.)

Miguel: Isabel! How did you know this number? You sixty-nined me? You getting crazy, girl!

Herbert: Star sixty-nine. It's a feature.

Miguel: What? Star sixty-nine? Coño. So Isabel, here's the deal with Toni, what I will do is tell her that we are planning something for spring and if she is interested in coming to Rutgers. She's probably asking somewhere between fifteen and twenty thousand. OK? So, I'll tell her we want her in the spring, we'll pick her up in Princeton in a limo, we'll sip on champagne and nibble on caviar. Ha, ha, ha. Tú me entiendes? The struggle continues. Oye, Isabel? What makes you such a witch? You called at the most opportune moment. When can you meet these gentlemen? Hallo? Hallo? *(To Herbert)* We got disconnected again.

(Miguel slams the phone against his leg.)

Herbert: No, please.

(Miguel talks to Adela again.)

Miguel: Adela! *(To Herbert, pointing across the street)* Look at that beautiful Puerto Rican lady. *(To Adela)* How's your son? Get my table and the mofongo ready, we're coming over for lunch.

Herbert: "Mofongo"? What's that?

Miguel: That my boy, is Puerto Rican soul food! Ha, ha, ha . . . It's delicious.

(As they walk away, Miguel notices Junior on the fire escape ladder. He's a forty-year-old, hard-core Puerto Rican, wearing a gold chain and a T-shirt of the boxer, Trinidad.)

Hey, Junior! What the fuck you doing up there? You've been there all this time?

Junior: Yep.

Miguel: I want you to meet . . . what's your name?

Herbert: Herbert.

Miguel: He's from the West Coast. He's Chicano.

Junior: Orale!

Miguel: That's right. He's here interviewing folks in Loisaida that were around in 1974. Maybe you can introduce him to some people? OK papi, we gotta go. You still on the program?

Junior: Yep.

(Miguel and Herbert exit. Junior comes down off the ladder.)

Este, 1974? Yeah, yeah , coño, they making me go way back. Let me think, uh, I was about eighteen years old. I used to wear Adidas. Este, los fros, the afros they used to be short, right? But in '74, they were like poof! Platform shoes, pigeon coups on the rooftops. Ah, diamond kites. Pet rocks and puca shells. The Latin Hustle, the Electric Boogie. Este, yeah, uh, rhyming and breaking was just getting started in the Bronx. Kool Herc was having block parties. Break it down, break it down!

(Lights change and Kurtis Blow's "Breaks" is heard. Junior starts break-dancing and locking. He injures his back slightly. The music stops. He slowly gets off the ground.)

Man, I ain't no Crazy Leggs! I'm gettin' too old for that shit. And then the salsa music was going on! Oh yeah, we would go dancing at Corso's, the Cheetah, the Red Parrot, the Palladium. Roberto Roena y su Apollo Sound, Bobby

Rodriguez y la Compañia, Eddie Palmieri, Ray Barreto, El Gran Combo, Ruben Blades was just starting out, Larry Harlow, he was Jewish, you know? And then there was Héctor, especially Héctor . . . "El cantante de los cantantes," Héctor Lavoe!

(Junior exits.
Lights change into a 1970s nightclub with disco ball. Héctor Lavoe enters in a white suit and microphone.)

Héctor:
> Tu amor es un periódico de ayer,
> Que nadie mas, preocura ya leer.
> Sensacional cuando salió en la madrugada,
> Al otro diá, ya noticia confirmada.
> En la tarde, materia olvidada,
> Tu amor es un periódico de ayer . . .

(Applause.)

Gracias mi gente. ¡Yo no llegué tarde, yo no llegué tarde, ustedes llegaron temprano! I'm very happy to be here, coño, I'm happy to be anywhere! Chévere, cheverinsky! Aquí les brindo mi son and who ever doesn't dance es porque tiene los zapatos rotos.

(A naked Streaker runs by.)

Ave María! Did you see that? Vieron eso? Oye ese loco, esta "streaking." Oye brother, I know it's hot, pero no joda, compay! Tiene el suit aire-condicionado. Y la sweater también. Chévere! . . . Quién es de Ponce?

(The Streaker runs by again.)

Streaker: I'm from Ponce, Héctor!
Héctor: ¡Ave María, el streaker es de Ponce también! Me cago en diez. ¡De ahí soy yo! Uds saben que yo los quiero de gratis. I love you y que Dios el todopoderoso los bendiga. Porque esto, aquí, está . . . *(Kiss)* "beautiful." Esto está chévere. Bien

nice. Riunite on ice. ¡Vaya! Chévere! Cheverinsky! *(Starts to laugh uncontrollably. He is high on drugs. He starts to weep)* ¿Perdóname mi gente, es que estoy fucking out of it, tú ve? ¿La vida loca, tú sabes? You have to enjoy life. Hay que gozar la vida porque . . .

> Todo tiene su final
> (Everything has it's end)
> Nada dura para siempre
> (Nothing lasts forever)
> Tenemos que recordar
> (We all have to realize)
> Que no existe la enternidad . . .
> (That enternity does not exist . . .)

(Blackout. Héctor exits.
Marvin Gaye's "Let's Get It On" is heard. Junior reenters.)

Junior: Back in 1974, there was a lot of fucking going on. A lot of beyaquera, crazy beyaquera! Tun, tun, tun, tun, baby! Sex everywhere, papi! That was before AIDS, before condoms, before Dominicans, you know? So the chocha was por todas partes, you couldn't get around it, tú sabes. Mira . . . the chocha estaba loca! ¡La chocha loca! Este . . . it was a wild, groovy . . . este chévere . . . uhm sexy, fuckin' wonderful era. And we were smokin' a lot of weed, getting high all the time. I used to sell loose joints, tabacco suelto.

¡I remember we used to say bajando! That's when the police, la jara, was driving down the street. Bajando . . .

(Miguel and Herbert reenter.)

Miguel: ¡Bajando! Baja . . .
Junior: Yo, not so loud . . . Shhhh . . .
All: Bajando . . . bajando . . . bajando . . .
Miguel: The main thing happening in '74, for me was the realization that the Lower East Side was like a bombed-out area.
Junior: I remember that's when they were throwing out the Puerto Ricans from the tenements, se puso caliente, olvídate.

Miguel: That's right. Meanwhile the Nuyorican poets, Piñero and CienFuegos, were hanging out at the Broome Street Bar at the corner of Broome Street and West Broadway.

Junior: All the Vietnam vets were coming back, because the war was pretty much over, and they were all strung-out on drugs, te acuerdas?

Miguel: Right. It was at this crucial moment in time that we were all becoming disoriented politically, on which way to go.

Herbert: What do you mean?

Miguel: I think the most important part about '74, young man, was the fact that I came to the realization that we were living in an age of no theories. No socialism, no communism. They had all fucked-up and died, so in an age of theory (or the lack of theory), there was nothing left but lust.

(Lights change. The Rolling Stones' "Doo Doo Doo Doo Doo (Heartbreaker)" is heard. Junior and Miguel exit. Herbert changes into Máximo Cólon, a Puerto Rican photographer and community activist.)

Máximo: The Movement saved my life. Back in the '70s I had a lot of fervor, a lot of passion. Still do. Many of my friends joined underground organizations. I worked aboveground as a photographer for the Movement.

I went to Manhattan City College and I remember being in a show called Dos Mundos, an exhibit of photographers from Puerto Rico and the U.S., and I had the only political stuff in the whole show. And a critic called me "a young, angry, venemous Puerto Rican photographer." I guess because I took photos of abandoned cars on the Lower East Side, and on the bottom I would write: "America: land of milk and honey." So I didn't get any shows after that! Ha, ha. No doubt.

I guess I have rebelled my whole life. I remember as a kid, my mother put me in Catholic school, and to me that was like the big cuckoo, you know? The boogeyman. And a nun had it out for me, a sister McDuff. I remember her pulling me out of line and she smacked me in the face. She smacked me in my face. So I ran back into the classroom, and you know those big rolls of butcher paper? The ones that have a big stick in the middle? Well, I pulled the stick out, ran back, and I hit her. I came back and hit her with a big stick! That's just the kind of person I am. I wasn't going to take shit from anyone, you know? I guess you could say that was my baptism into armed struggle. "Liberation Theology." No doubt.

I am heavily inspired by Los Independientistas and the Nationalists. People like Don Pedro Albizu Campos. This goes way back to the '30s and the '40s. And in 1950 there was an insurrection in Jayuya, Puerto Rico, where the National got bombed. Don Pedro is arrested, and the Nationalists took up arms against the government. So we have that history like an inspiration for us. Lolita Lebrón, Rafael Cancel Miranda, Irving Flores and Andrés Cordero, they sacrificed. They said: "Yo, Truman, we don't like what's happening."

They stormed the U.S. Congress and said: "This ain't gonna go down like that," and they shot the place up. They spent twenty-eight years in jail for that. Twenty-eight years. The sacrifice. I have a lot of admiration for these people— the men and women willing to die for their autonomy, their independence, la liberación de Puerto Rico.

We have to fight the U.S. occupation and bombing of the civilian island of Vieques, where they hold Puerto Rican prisoners and then ship them to Hartford. Yet these so-called political prisoners are not considered prisoners of war, therefore negating any rights guaranteed to them under the Geneva Convention.

Why can't the FALN come to the bargaining table in Washington, like Mandela, like Arafat, like the IRA? They were once called "terrorists" too. It's because Puerto Rico is treated as a domestic issue where international law does not apply. It's because we are people of color. It's a pathological relationship between colonizer and colonized. They are not political prisoners, they are, in fact, prisoners of war.

I recently went and took photos at the Puerto Rican Day Parade. And I swear it was like we were one big family out there. And you know what connected us all? The flag. The

Puerto Rican flag. And I saw people waving that flag, wearing that flag, relating to that flag. Knowing the importance of that flag. Now I know you might not care about Lolita, you might not care about Albizu, or whether Puert Rico is free or not. But I just want to remind you that the next time you wave that flag, that there were people willing to sacrifice their lives for that flag. La bandera Puertoriqueña.

(A large Puerto Rican flag unfurls across the stage. "Que Bonita Bandera" is heard. Máximo recites the names of the Puerto Rican prisoners released in 1999.)

Haydee Beltrán. Presente!
Edwin Cortés. Presente!
Elizam Escobar. Presente!
Ricardo Jiménez. Presente!
Adolfo Matos. Presente!
Antonio Camacho Negrón. Presente!
Alejandrina Torres. Presente!
Carlos Alberto Torres. Presente!
Oscar López Rivera. Presente!
Alberto Rodríguez. Presente!
Ida Luz Rodríguez. Presente!
Alicia Rodríguez. Presente!
Jaun Cegarra Palmar. Presente!
Dylcia Pagán. Presente!
Luis Rosa. Presente!
José Solíz. Presente!
Carmen Valentín. Presente!
Qué viva Puerto Rico libre!

(Lolita Lebrón black-and-white newsreel footage is projected on the flag. After the footage is shown, black exploitation music is heard.)

Voice-Over: Look out Cleopatra Jones, step aside Charlie's Angels. There's a new super barrio hero in town. Straight out of the Loisaida—it's Becky Boriqua!

(Becky Boriqua enters. She is dressed in a fatigue jacket, bell-bottom jeans and a large afro.)

Becky: I am Becky Boriqua, soul sister and defender of the barrio! The only thing I hate more than junkies and state-hooders is honky pigs!

(Commissioner O'Hara, a corrupt Irish cop, enters.)

O'Hara: Top o' the mornin' to ya, Becky.
Becky: It's that cracker, Commissioner O'Hara.
O'Hara: Trying to be Angie Dickinson again are ya? Listen sister, why don't you go back to the projects and make fried pla-tanos for your five half-and-half mulatto children, and leave the dangerous police work to racist, um, I mean Irish cops like me. Now scram, beat it, adios before I make cuchifrito outta ya!

(O'Hara exits. Mofongo Man enters. He is dressed in a '70s pimp outfit with a gigantic oily afro.)

Mofongo Man: ¡Oye, Becky Boriqua! ¡Aquí está tu papi, baby!
Becky: Oh shit, it's Mofongo Man!

(O'Hara pops his head in.)

O'Hara: This Nuyorican is a bad mother . . .
Becky: Shut your mouth!

(Mofongo Man sings to the music of Curtis Mayfield's "Pusher-man":)

Mofongo Man:
> I'm your brother
> I'm your pusher
> I'm your Rican
> In the alley
> Have some coke
> Have some weed
> I'm Mofongo Man

All: He's Mofongo Man.

Mofongo Man: My afro is made out of mofongo, dig. I got toxic garlic juices drippin' down the side of my face. The shit is gonna go down, nena!

Becky: Mofongo Man! This hustle is over papi and I'm gonna have to make chuletas outta your ass! But don't you fuck up my nails or my outfit.

Mofongo Man: Oh c'mon negrita, you ain't gotta be so coooold. You're acting like that lesbian Angela Davis and shit.

Becky: Why are you selling junk to our brothers and sisters? Don't you care about the children and the free-lunch program?

Mofongo Man: Free lunch? How about free base? Hee, hee.

Becky: Why are you fronting for the mob and the government? It's a conspiracy. Mofongo Man. C.O.I.N.T.E.L.P.R.O. Bro!

(Mofongo Man lights up a joint.)

Mofongo Man: You wanna hit, Becky Bacalao?

Becky: I'll give you a hit!! *(Hits Mofongo Man)*

Mofongo Man: Ouch! Ain't that a bitch! I'm gonna have to teach you a lesson, mami.

(Mofongo Man grabs his afro and squeezes toxic garlic juices into Becky's eyes.)

Becky: AAAAAAGGH! You blinded me. I got mojo de ajo in my ojo! *(Tastes the garlic)* Damn, that shit is good! Can I get some arroz with that? Aaahhh!

(O'Hara enters.)

O'Hara: Sweet mother of blue-eyed Jesus! What happened to ya, Becky?

Becky: I'm blind! I'm blind as José Feliciano!

(José Feliciano's theme song to Chico and the Man *is heard briefly.)*

That was stupid! But you must help me, commissioner!

O'Hara: Oh no child, I'm in cahoots with Mofongo Man, I protect him! He does whatever I say. Right? Riverdance for me, negro!

(Mofongo Man dances a quick Irish jig with music. O'Hara and Mofongo Man share a sinister laugh. They freeze.)

Voice-Over: Is this the end for our good sister Becky Boriqua?

Becky *(To the audience)*: Luckily, I brought my eye drops from my tia's botanica—limpia ojo de ajo or ajo de ojo—whatever! And now I must call upon the Yoruba Spirits to help me with Mofongo Man's evil ways!

(Jungle drums are heard. Becky, in a spell, begins a chant.)

> Rita Moreno . . . Chita Rivera
> Jennifer López . . . Qué tremendas
> ¡Nalgas! La vida loca . . .
> What a piece of caca . . .

(Breaking out of the spell) I got some ass to whoop!

(Becky beats up O'Hara and Mofongo Man to the beat of old-school funk music. O'Hara exits.)

Mofongo Man: That's it nena, I'm gonna give you a double-barrel dose of my mojo de ajo!

(Mofongo Man throws garlic juice toward Becky. She quickly puts on special fried-green plantain sunglasses.)

Becky: It's a good thing I remembered to bring my tostón sunglasses to soak up the deadly juices de Mofongo Man!

Mofongo Man: Damn!

(They fight in a stylized slow-motion manner. Becky lands a right hook.)

Coño!

(Mofongo Man grabs Becky's breast.)

Que rico!

Becky: That's it. You gonna pay!

(Strobe light slow-motion effect. Becky kicks Mofongo Man in the nuts. She also takes off his toxic, dripping wig and throws it into his face.)

Mofongo Man: Ahhhhh! I'm melting!

(Mofongo Man exits.)

Becky: I am Becky Boriqua, Independientista and righteous soul sister. Defending life, liberty, justice and the Nuyorican way! And now I have to go clean up the Bronx! Qué viva la mujer. Damn—I broke a nail! *(Exits)*

(Olgie, a middle-aged community activist, enters.)

Olgie: Yesterday, my son, who is sixteen years old says to me, "Mom I'm not going to school today." And I said, "Yes you are." And he says, "They're just gonna kill us, they will say we are junkies and that we have no hope. They are gonna shoot us in the street."

And I thought, Who's he talking about? The gangs? What?

He was scared to death. He was talking about the cops. And I thought, My God, I have to do something right here— my sixteen-year-old son thinks the police are going to kill him!

When I was sixteen I became a Young Lord. When I was sixteen, I said, "Oh shit—Revolution!" At sixteen, I started learning about Marx and Lenin and class struggle. I was just a kid but I got involved. We weren't flower children we were more R&B because I grew up in a black neighborhood. That was the southeast Bronx. 166th Street and Boston Road.

I have to admit that at age sixteen, I was also very into the fashion—Fred Michael shoes, alpaca sweaters, suede suits. And with the makeup I was Twiggy and the hair feathered-back like Farrah, and eyelashes like Mia Farrow. Imagine, a Boriqua Mia Farrow who was a Young Lord.

We were instrumental in getting young people's energies geared toward doing something positive like the breakfast program, clothing drives, T.B. testing, and we did education too.

At age sixteen, I was helping to organize the gangs not to fight each other. These two gangs were having this war one day. I remember, the Black Spades and the Viceroys were on the building rooftops throwing Molotov cocktails from one building to another. And I reacted because a baby's crib caught on fire. It exploded actually. I got really enraged and I didn't bother to think about my own safety and I just shot up those stairs to the top of the building and I yelled, "I wanna talk to the War Lord, I wanna talk to the War Lord!" I didn't realize they could have thrown me off the freakin' roof! So, the War Lord came up and said, "Who are you?" And I said, "I live in this building and I just saw a baby's crib explode and catch on fire—it could of had the baby in there! It could of been your own cousin, it could of been your sister's baby, and you wouldn't have known! How could you do this to your own people?"

And then they said, "We can throw you off the roof right now, bitch!"

But I remembered, I had my Young Lord's beret, so I put it on. And I said, "You will have to contend with the Young Lords." They saw my button, they had known about us in the papers because the cops were bad-mouthing us.

By this time, some of the other Young Lords had made it to the roof where I was. The War Lord said let's listen to what these brothers and sisters have to say, and eventually we got the two opposing War Lords together and we pow-wowed. And we brought about a truce. We saved a few lives.

We lived in a collective in those projects, in that war zone. I know it. I was only sixteen and I was just reacting. They never did throw me off that roof.

By late '74, early '75, it was all totally dismantled. The Lords completely scattered, some went to Philly some went back to Chicago and some to New Jersey. I sacrificed eight years of my life you know, and that was twenty-four-seven. I am very proud of that.

Many Young Lords incorporated back into society, some have become judges, lawyers, political pundits. One Young Lord even became Geraldo Rivera. Some Lords stayed grass-roots and are still involved in the Movement.

I still work at changing this freakin' system everyday you know—as a social worker, a parent community activist. Palante, siempre palante, as my good friend Iris says. She's a filmmaker. You should talk to her. I have to stay positive for my children and set an example.

(Olgie's teenage son enters.)

Because I am still an idealist. But I am not a romantic. The romance was gone years ago, baby. Some people say, "Olgie you are paranoid." I'm not paranoid. I tell them I'm from the South Bronx, you naci en el sur de Bronx! You can call me paranoid but it's not really a word in my vocabulary. And if you are so smart then you tell me this, what do you say to your child when he thinks Mayor Giuliani is going to freakin' kill him? *(Pause)* That's all.

(Olgie exits. A merengue song is heard. Mayor Giuliani enters, dancing and shaking the audience's hands. He crosses the stage, pulls out a gun and shoots Olgie's teenage son. Mayor Giuliani exits. Blackout.

After a beat, Yoruba drums and chants are heard. In light shadow, the teenager slowly gets up and walks off into the afterlife.

Lights up. Miguel, wearing a cast on his right arm, enters his apartment. He carries a typewriter with great struggle. He puts it down on the table, and starts typing with his left hand.)

Miguel: Dear Mister Mayor . . . Your policies . . . are killing our youth . . .

(A knock at the door.)

Come in, it's open!

(Herbert enters.)

Herbert: Hola, Miguel.

Miguel: Hey, uh . . .

Herbert: Herbert.

Miguel: Yes, of course. Have you had luck with the people I told you to interview?

Herbert: Yes, thank you. Hey, Miguel, what happened to your hand?

Miguel: Did you hear the story?

Herbert: Junior told me you tried to be a hero or something?

Miguel: No, I didn't try to be a Arnold Schwarzenegger! I had just returned from my lecture and book tour, when I was driving in my truck around Loisaida. And I see these white guys beating on a white woman. My black friends were standing around saying, "Beat the white bitch, beat the white bitch! Go ahead you're all white, kill yourselves, motherfuckers!" My attitude was, "I know you guys from childhood, what the fuck are you doing? If it was your sister, your mother, you would step in, you know?"

So I rolled down my window and said, "Yo." So I parked my truck on the side and I'm helping her up from the floor. They had been kicking her in the face. One guy decided to give her one last swipe and she said, "Watch out!" I thought the guy was coming for me, but he wasn't. He was going to open up her face because he had a razor blade between his fingers. So my left hand went up and he caught my middle finger, the tendon. And then she said, "You saved my life." But the bitch took off running. And the guys took off in a car with Jersey plates.

So it must have been a drug hustle. But the funny part was, that my middle finger was standing up in the "fuck you" position. And at that point, the cops came by and they said, "Who the fuck you think you are insulting us like that? We'll arrest your fucking ass."

And I said, "You get out of the car and make my finger go down." So he got out of the car and brought the finger down and the finger went—pop—right back up. Instead of them saying, "Let's take you to a hospital," they said, "Get your truck out of the way before we give you three tickets."

I was so traumatized that instead of getting in my truck and driving myself to the hospital, which is seventeen blocks away, I walked.

Herbert: You walked?

Miguel: I walked! I'm walking down the street, my finger is in the "fuck you" position. Everybody is walking around me because I'm dripping blood, you know. And I get to the hospital and the nurses turn pallid. And the first thing out of my mouth is: "You have to be careful, my blood is tainted, my blood is tainted." So everybody ran for gloves, ha, ha, ha! I had three weeks downtime, but it became a rebirth. It teaches you a lot of humility to wipe your ass with the left hand and get your fingers full of shit! Ha, ha, ha!

Herbert: Where did this happen?

Miguel: This happened on Sixth Street and Avenue A. The police presence has been stepped-up because it's so gentrified now. They got a French restaurant on the corner, a fucking bistro on Avenue B! Hello, Avenue B! But the food is out of this world! It's delicious! Cooked by Mexicans. Ha, ha, ha. See, back in the day, white people would never cross First Avenue to the Lower East Side. Nevah!

Herbert: Never?

Miguel: Nevah!

Herbert: Jesus.

(Miguel and Herbert exit. Junior appears through an open window.)

Junior: And now you got these blanquitos, these grungers, taking over Loisaida. These motherfuckers come from Connecticut, Maine and Vermont. ¡La punta de la pinga! I'm Nuyorican, *original* (Spanish). I grew up in the motherfuckin' Bellevue. And the extent of my education was living in the streets. ¡Porque yo me metí en todo! I did it all. I ran with the whole fuckin' drug culture. I began doing drugs when I was ten, smoking weed. By seventeen I started banging

bombitas. I got in touch with the demons, and it got to the point where I started banging in my neck. I was trying to take myself out of here, faster. Shit, I even went through the whole thing of hustling for drugs. Okay, suck my dick, pay me. ¿Yo me saco la bichuela pero tú me tienes que dar algo, viste? It got to a point when I even lived with a guy. And you know what was funny about that? Was with the homeboys, right, you couldn't let them know you were doing this shit. But the homeboys, it turned out, that these mother-fuckers were doing the same thing!

One time I was with a homo, and one of my homeboys, a real macho guy comes in and he didn't know I was inside the crib, so I peeked through the bedroom door, and I said, "Ooh shit that's homeboy," I was about to say something else but I said, nah. So I'm clocking him, right. Before I knew it, this maricón estaba—butt-fucking him, on the motherfuckin' refrigerator, allí 'staba, uhhhh . . . uhhhh . . . uhhhh. I said, "Oooh shit!"

Now the whole thing about being with men is that when I was getting high, they were there for me like friends, companionship. They were there to help me do the right thing.

I'm a survivor, bro, because I know who I am. I'm black, Spanish and Native American. I have all three and you have to connect with all three. I don't subscribe to Hispanic, but I can't deny that they raped our culture. I remember one time, I was in this behavioral modification program. It was called "Su Casa." Now it was called Su Casa but you weren't suppose to speak Spanish. *Su Casa.* One day they said: "All Hispanics up against the wall." I didn't move, and one of the brothers says to me, "Hey Junior, they said all Hispanics up against the wall." And I said, "I'm not Hispanic." He says, "You speak Spanish, don't you?" I said, "I speak English too, but I'm not British!" I shut that motherfucker up right there, know what I mean? Who you kidding? Yo soy Taíno, I have Yoruba spirits in my veins.

(Yoruba music and chants are heard. Lights slowly fade on Junior.

Lights come up on the street corner. Nuyorican street poet, Pedro Pietri, enters, reciting a poem and hanging black paintings on the wall. He also carries signs that read: POEMS FOR ONE DOLLAR and LEGALIZE MARIJUANA.)

Pietri:

    Juan
    Miguel
    Milagros
    Olga
    Manuel
    will right now be doing their own thing
    where beautiful people sing
    and dance and work together
    where the wind is a stranger
    to miserable weather conditions
    where you do not need a dictionary
    to communicate with your people
    aquí se habla Español all the time
    aquí you salute your flag first

aquí there are no Dial soap commercials
aquí everybody smells good
aquí TV dinners do not have a future
aquí the men and women admire desire
and never get tired of each other
aquí que pasa power is what's happening
aquí to be called negrito
means to be called *love.*

(Ric and Richard enter as themselves. Pietri is unaware of them.)

Richard: That was "Puerto Rican Obituary," right?

(Pietri turns around.)

Pietri: Wow, how did you know that, man?
Richard: That's a classic. My father told me about that poem.
Pietri: Who's your father, man?
Richard: José Montoya.
Pietri: José Mon— Great man! Great! Ha, ha, ha! Coño, I know your dad, man. He's with the Royal Chicano Air Force. Yeah man, I met your dad on the Lower East Side with Miguel Piñero. He's a great poet. Send my regards to your pops.
Richard: I sure will.
Pietri: Yeah, the Chicanos hung out with us Nuyoricans back in '74.
Ric: Why was 1974 such a good year?
Pietri: It wasn't such a good year, man. '71 was better. By 1974, there was acute paranoia, no one trusted anybody. All these fantastic movements, all these progressive ideas played out. Everybody withdrew. Then we saw the emergence of the Nuyorican Poets Movement. All the political bullshit ended and the cultural nationalists came into focus and twenty-five years later we're still around. Have you gone to the Nuyorican Café?
Richard: We're going to a poetry slam there tonight. What do you think of these new slams?
Pietri: I think they're bullshit. You know. You get up there and read and then there's these judges grading you from one to ten. And it's become national, very popular. I don't know

why. One time, they made me a judge and I gave everyone a zero. Ha, ha, ha! I slammed them, you know!

Ric: Are these your paintings?

Pietri: Yeah man, that's my "dark series."

Ric: They're all black.

Pietri: That's very perceptive of you man. Ha, ha, ha! Yeah, they're all black. I paint them all black. If people give me their portraits, I paint black over them. *(Pause)* See, I always wear black, that's because, I'm dead.

Richard: You're dead?

Pietri: That's right. I was killed in Vietnam during the Tet Offensive. See, my father was a Puerto Rican nationalist and my mother was a Republican, so I had this fucked-up loyalty towards America. So I went to Vietnam, and I realized that we were not there to help, we were there to kill, to rape, to maim. So I got killed, but I refused to die.

Ric: Do you consider yourself a Nuyorican or a Puerto Rican?

Pietri: Both. Hey, by the way I got your Puerto Rican passports right here, from the Puerto Rican embassy.

(Pietri gives Ric and Richard handmade passports.)

Richard: Puerto Rican passports? Far out.

Ric: The Puerto Rican embassy? It doesn't really exist, right?

Pietri *(Angry)*: It does exist, man! What's wrong with you? See, it's that defeatist attitude that keeps us in this limbo welfare state. Fuck it, we're free! In order to be free, we have to start thinking free. Dig?

Ric: Dig.

(Tense moment.)

Pietri: Ha, ha, ha! You guys want some of this smoke?

Ric: No.

Pietri: Good, more for me.

(Richard lights Pietri's joint.)

See, I got glaucoma from 'Nam, so I gotta smoke weed for medicinal purposes. But, even if I didn't have glaucoma, I'd still smoke weed. Ha, ha, ha! Hey, you guys want to hear another poem?

Richard: Yeah.

Pietri: It'll cost you a dollar. Give me a dollar, man.

Richard: All I have is this ten.

(Pietri snatches the ten from Richard's hand.)

Pietri: That's good.

Free grass for the working class—Don't let the system kick your ass.

Free grass for the working class—Don't let the system kick your ass.

The only sane person in NYC is Alex the Green Can from Latin Manhattan and Greece: street vendor of hot dogs and sausages and pretzels and shish kebab on lonely stick and knishes and cans of soda too, to keep you cool in hell, also known as New York City!

(They exit. Lights slowly fade.

Lou Reed's "Heroin" is heard. Junior's apartment. He opens a window and lights his cigarrette lighter. He looks at the flame, in a reflective mood.)

Junior: I am forty-two years old, papa, forty-two. Este . . . and people say: Coño, you're forty-two, bro? And you did all that? And you did time? And you did drugs? And you used to shoot? And you got no tattoos? No scars? I got my teeth. A lot of fiends don't have their teeth. I'm clean now. I have a passion for life. I work as a holistic health coordinator, pure grassroots, baby. We, uhm, do needle exchange, pass out condoms, safe-sex info. Because these kids now, are killing themselves. I see so many young, white dope fiends coming into the clinic. I'm going to help them. I'll help you motherfucker and your white ass better listen to me, or else you die!

(Junior closes the window. Lights fade.
Lights up on Miguel's apartment. He enters, followed by Herbert
reading from a book.)

Herbert:
>we joked once, Piñero,
>on Nuyorican streets
>while visions fused
>a world of biting sounds

Herbert and Miguel:
>weaving Chicano-Boriqua
>tales of survival

Herbert:
>as hungered denizens
>careened through Loisaida avenues,
>each pair of eyes
>not able to match
>the intensity of Mikey
>spiking madness
>into another day of survival

Herbert and Miguel:
>weaving Chicano-Boriqua
>tales of survival

Herbert:
>Simón que yes, carnal
>of the fiery pen
>and pensive eyes
>which bore into our consciousness,
>the truth hurts, but the pain
>is one of growth and knowing . . .

Herbert and Miguel: Adiós, Mickey, adiós . . .

(Herbert closes the book.)

Miguel: Ricardo Sánchez, a Chicano brother from Corpus Christi.
Herbert: Rest in peace.
Miguel: Another one, yes. You know the week he read that at the Café we couldn't get Ginsberg and Burroughs off the stage. Ha, ha, ha. *(Pause)* Look, I got to get down to Princeton young man. When do you go back to the Coast?
Herbert: Tomorrow.
Miguel: Well, you tell José Montoya that the Nuyoricans are still here, and tell him Chicano Power!
Herbert: Bajando . . .
Miguel: Bajando . . . What's your favorite Puerto Rican soul food?
Herbert: Mofongo!

(They hug.)

Thanks for everything Miguel, adiós.

(Herbert is about to exit.)

Miguel: Herbert!
Herbert *(Surprised)*: You remembered my name.
Miguel: Listen, there was one last thing I wanted to share with you about Miguel Piñero . . .

(Herbert reaches for his tape recorder.)

No. Just listen. The day Miguel got paid fifteen thousand for the transfer of *Short Eyes* from the Public to the Beaumont, he went to the bank and put twelve thousand cash in his pocket. Literally . . . Then he came downtown and gave everyone one-hundred-dollar bills. To all the little old ladies, the little kids. And I stopped him and said, "Where are you going?" "I'm going to cop," he said. And I said, "Why? Now that you have money—the rich addicts, the white addicts have it delivered." So we went to my apartment, and had it delivered. We copped and he got high. And Miguel said, "I can't do this, this is not fun. I can't have this shit delivered. I got to go out there, and shoot it up in the abandoned buildings. I have to go back to the streets—that's where the *danger* is." The danger, you understand? Success didn't change that crazy, brilliant motherfucker one bit!

(The guitar solo from "Heroin" is heard. Then the sound of wind. The lights change. A silhouetted figure of a man in a long leather jacket and short afro enters. It is Miguel Piñero.)

Piñero *(Voice-over):*

    Just once before I die
    I want to climb up on a

tenement sky
to dream my lungs out till I cry
then scatter my ashes thru
the Lower East Side . . .

(Piñero slowly walks downstage center. He kneels down and lifts his shirt sleeve, revealing a tattoo on his forearm. Herbert and Miguel move close to him.)

All: Mi Vida Loca.

(Santana's "Samba Pa Ti" is reprieved. Distant police sirens are heard. Slow fade to black.)

The End

Mission Magic
Mystery Tour

SAN FRANCISCO

For Ronnie Burke
ACT UP/San Francisco

ACKNOWLEDGMENTS

Culture Clash thanks the following people for their support of this production: Ellen Gavin, Omar Sosa, Greg Landau, Stacy and Dr. Loco, Alma del Barrio, the family of Rodrigo Reyes for the usage of his poetry, René Yañez, Sal García, Jack Wicker, The Boat House, the San Francisco Mime Troupe, Jim González, César Ascarrunz, José and Brian from Andorra Inn, Don Bajema, the family of Eva García, RAP, Ronnie Burke, ACT UP/San Francisco, SF Cannabis Club, Betita Martínez and Maria de Colombia.

Introduction to
MISSION MAGIC MYSTERY TOUR

By Marcelo Rodríguez

There are two constants about San Francisco's Mission District that have been true ever since Junípero Serra built his northernmost Spanish Catholic outpost that gave the neighborhood its name. The first is that the Mission is forever changing. The second is that all change in the Mission is accompanied by anguished complaints about how much better things were before.

Of course, this could pretty well describe virtually every place on earth where more than one person gathers. But in the Mission, this constant clash is unusual in one way: it fully exposes the area's always juicy and often bizarre idiosyncrasies, making the tempestuous neighborhood a great source of offbeat humor. And there's probably no one better at exploiting this than the Mission-born Culture Clash.

Richard Montoya, Ricardo Salinas and Herbert Siguenza don't hang out in the neighborhood as much since they moved Culture Clash to Los Angeles twelve years ago. But they do come "home" often to inspect the changes and soak up the humor. The players are slightly different. Parking is harder to come by. The rhythms of hip-hop and techno-merengue have replaced salsa and punk rock. The ghetto blasters now fit inside the ear. A tiny one-bedroom apartment today costs $1,500 a month. And the *Chronicle* has finally learned you can get a good meal in the Mission and not get mugged for dessert.

Still, the founder of Culture Clash, the indefatigable René Yañez, continues to live in the neighborhood battling the housing pressures and promoting great art. The latter day Central American Juniperos, with their nonstop Biblia-thumping, are still louder than the Muni buses on 24th and Mission. You can still find good weed, a Che Guevara T-shirt and plenty of DON'T PRAY IN MY SCHOOLS AND I WON'T THINK IN YOUR CHURCH bumper stickers in the neighborhood. And, while you will never taste a better burrito anywhere else in the world, you still *cannot* find a decent pupusa.

What sets *Mission Magic Mystery Tour* apart from Culture Clash's other site-specific shows is a deep sense of the personal. And because this neighborhood belongs to Culture Clash as much as it does to the now-unemployed dot.com-ers (who somehow can still afford the high rents they themselves created), the three were able to reach deep inside and, as importantly, into their own past, to mine the comedy and the bittersweet truths that come with change.

In Miami, Culture Clash's pointed jabs were directed at always melancholy and often delusional Cuban exiles. Here, they take aim at the Bolivian, César Ascarrunz, the perennial mayoral candidate in whose notorious Latin Palace the Clashers drank many a beer.

In San Diego, immigrant Asians and their lowriding two-toned Acuras take some digs. In *Mission Magic Mystery Tour*, an aging Chicano pays a visit to reminisce about his Impala lowrider cruising the Mission Street of Montoya, Salinas and Siguenza's teenage years, and revives an old beef with a puritanical Dianne Feinstein, complete, of course, with Malo's "Suavecito" playing in the background.

It's hard to find a Nuyorican street poet wandering on 16th Street, but there's an abundance of visionary verse here from the late theatrical director Rodrigo Reyes and the brilliant writer Don Bajema, both of them close friends of the Clash.

Just like every other progressive Latino in San Francisco in the 1980s, the members of Culture Clash were less than happy with the maddeningly contradictory poses of former Supervisor Jim González (for a time, the only "Hispanic" elected official in the city). Was he a liberal Latino? A corporate lapdog? In a riotous "Where Are They Now?" news flash, González pops up as a lobbyist for the dot.com interests, as enigmatic as ever. González's pretzel defense of all things dot.com is actually presented by both Montoya and Salinas when speaking to each other on cell phones: the hyper politician is still too wild to be played by a single mere actor.

While the rest of the world may find Siguenza's Adelita, Montoya's Maria and Salinas's Berta exceedingly kooky, that's not a problem for Culture Clash. These homeboys *are* Adelita, Maria and Berta.

Mission Magic Mystery Tour not only proves that you can come home again, but that while you're there, you may as well poke fun at it—and at yourself. The Mission is basically the same place Culture Clash left twelve years ago. All complaints aside, it is still the heart and artistic soul of San Francisco. And it's a good thing that, just like Rodrigo Reyes, Culture Clash is not really gone. They are still here, among us, walking in the Mission.

Marcelo Rodríguez *is a writer, editor, journalist and entrepreneur who lives in San Francisco.*

PRODUCTION HISTORY

Mission Magic Mystery Tour was commissioned by BRAVA! for Women in the Arts. It premiered at the Eureka Theatre in San Francisco in the winter of 2001. The director was Max Ferrá; the set design was by Loy Arcenas; the lighting design was by Kate Boyd; the sound design was by Culture Clash, B. C. Keller and John A. Murphy; the costume design was by Culture Clash; video was by Lourdes Portillo; the dramaturg was Max Ferrá; the production manager was Jennifer Figueroa; the technical director was Lisa Hori-Garcia; the prop masters were Alexis Williams and Norma Hernández and the stage manager was Bert van Aalsburg.

The voice of Jack Kerouac is heard as lights slowly come up onstage.

The Voice of Jack Kerouac:
There was a little alley in San Francisco
back of the Southern Pacific
station at Third and Townsend
in redbrick of drowsy lazy afternoons
with everybody at work in offices
in the air you feel the impending rush of their
        commuter frenzy
as soon they'll be charging en masse
from Market and Sansome buildings
on foot and in buses and all well dressed
thru workingman Frisco . . .

(A fog horn is heard. A low fog covers the stage. Dr. Loco's "Barrio Mission" is heard, as the Voice of Kerouac fades out. A woman who sells roses enters and sits down.)

all you San Franciscos will have to fall eventually and
        burn again.

(Another fog horn is heard. A video image of the Virgin Mary and falling roses is projected onstage. Two Latino men—Jim 1 and Jim 2—enter wearing suits, carrying suitcases and talking to each other on their cell phones. They never stop moving.)

Jim 1: The dot.com-ers are here to stay!

Jim 2: The dot.com-ers aren't going anywhere, pal.

Jim 1: The protesters, the pissed-off artists, aren't going to stop them. The anti-dot.com-ers have shown some organizational abilities. They have shown that there is a real fear in the Mission. A fear that has frankly, been here a long time. Now that they have tapped into that fear what have they done? They got six hundred people to a protest, a bunch of press clippings and a few supervisors got elected. But if a kid says to me, "What have you done for me lately?" I can say two things: "Here kid, here's a bunch of press clippings," or I can say, "Here's a job at Flowers.com."

Jim 2: For the last five to seven years, a lot of yuppies have moved to the Mission. They moved here because the rent was cheap. But now they're afraid. Because the rents have quadrupled. Ha ha ha! Guess what yuppie? You've become a Latino! They're one of us now! Because now they live with the same fear that every Latino family has ever lived with. And guess what yuppie? Welcome to the neighborhood fucker!

Jim 1: They are the new NIMBY.

Jim 2: Not In My Backyard!

Jim 1: Right! It used to be an old grumpy German guy. Now, it's a twenty-eight year old, who is suddenly saying . . .

Jim 2: "I will not have Latinos replaced!"

Jim 1: Because if they're replaced, *my* rent is going to go up!

Jim 2: Welcome to the Mission fuckers!

Flower Lady: Me llamo Rosa. Tengo veinte años vendiendo flores. Salgo todo los días a vender, menos el lunes. Me levanto a las seis de la mañana, salgo de la casa y tomo el catorce Misión para el centro donde está el Flower Mart. Y allí, compro rosas mas que todo. Compro como siete docenas. Y gasto entre quince a veinti-cinco dólares. De ahí vuelvo, a mi casa donde las lavo, les quito algunas hojas, las corto, porque están muy largas y las separo una por una. De ahí, las envuelvo con plástico, las pongo su listoncito rojo, y salgo a venderlas una rosa por dos dólares o la media docena por diez.

Jim 2: The dot.com-ers are in the Mission because they bought the old warehouses that nobody wanted. These X-ers and

Y-ers have been all over the world, they don't want stale gringo food. No! Here in the Mission they got their Thai, Indian, Mexican . . .

Jim 1: Cambodian . . .

Jim 2: Salvadorean food. So you got this pierced, tattooed, thinking out of the box work force, and at the end of the day, they want to be in the artistic part of the city. They don't want to live in San Jose. Or god forbid . . .

Jim 1: Fucking Fremont!

Flower Lady: Empiezo en la calle veinte-cuatro y voy a la Iglesia San Pedro donde agarro gente que está saliendo de la misa de la mañana. Entro a las tiendas, como La Victoria, Discolandia, Casa Sánchez y allí los dueños y los clientes me compran algo. Y así, toda la mañana, me voy por toda la Misión. Como las doce, me regreso a la casa, como un poquito, hago mis mandaditos y como las tres, recojo los niños de la escuela y los llevo a la casa. Ahí ven sus muñequitos en la televisión y hacen sus tareas. Salgo a vender al BART, aprovechando los trabajadores que vienen del centro.

Jim 2: I can't hear you, Jim.

Jim 1: Switch to Sprint!

Flower Lady: La renta me lo han subido bastante. Varios de mis vecinos, ya no pudieron pagar la renta, y se fueron para Richmond, mejor. Mucha gente se está yendo para Richmond. Dicen que allí está mas barato, pero hay muchos Negros. Ahora los que se están mudando a la Misión son Americanos, jóvenes, vienen de todas partes. Vienen de Colorado, no se porque. Como que aquí hay trabajos para ellos, verdad. Pero me está costando quedarme aquí, voy a tener que meter los niños en un cuarto, y rento el otro. No sé como voy a hacer. Sólo Dios sabrá.

Jim 1: They want flats and lofts in the sunny, exotic Mission and they will pay top dollar for them. And, you know what people are saying?

Jim 2: What?

Jim 1: "Holy fuck, my neighborhood is changing!" Now, we have taxis on Valencia Street!

Jim 2: We got valet parking on Mission Street!

Jim 1: All of a sudden, we have gringos walking around with attitude. These Banana Republicans are partying, screaming, peeing in the streets 'til four in the morning. The other day, I was talking in Spanish, and I'm getting this look. And I'm thinking, wait a minute, this is my neighborhood, I was born here, how dare you give me attitude, fucker!

Jim 2: That's how it was ten years ago when the Chinos came in and bought half the Mission.

Jim 1: Chinos cabrones!

Jim 2: And before that, it was the war-torn Nicaraguans and Salvadoreans, those pupusa eating motherfuckers!

Flower Lady: Hey!

Jim 2: Sorry señora. And before that, the Irish and Germans were here. Fuck me, the Spanish were the first to invade the Mission, thank you very much! And I'm sure the indios weren't thrilled about that! Father Junípero Serra was the first developer. Father Junípero Serra was the first Joe O'Donohue. You see ese, history shows us that people who come to San Francisco from other places, always come to the Mission first.

Flower Lady: Vine de El Salvador, sóla, como mataron a mi esposo allá durante la guerra civil. Y yo vine con las ilusión de que aquí era bonito como Beverly Hills, Disneylandia, verdad. Como así veíamos allá en la televisión. El *Baywatch*. Yo no creía que había miseria aquí en Los Estados Unidos. Pero sí lo hay, viera.

Jim 1: The fact is, we old fuckers blew it. The so-called economic development agencies in the Mission didn't have the vision to buy their own buildings. And now they're screaming bloody murder.

Jim 2: It was because we were stoned through the '60s and '70s. We could have bought those old buildings for a song, and today we'd be the owners renting to the dot.commies.

Jim 1: Com-ers.

Jim 2: Whatever.

Jim 1: We could have bought the Armory, the Red Stone Building, the Woman's Building.

Jim 2: Well, I'm the one who secured the bond for the BRAVA Theater. Did you know that?

Jim 1: You did?

Jim 2: That's right. All our hands are bloody. Nobody's innocent here.

Flower Lady: Al escurecer, vuelvo a la casa y les doy de cenar a los niños. Les reviso sus tareas, y se acuestan a las nueve. Y ahí es cuando aprovecho a salir a los bares. Antes vendía más rosas porque entraba a las cantinas Mexicanas. Pero como hoy se han convertido en bares de Americanos, pues a veces no me dejan entrar. Bien pesados los hombres, me dicen bien feo, me ultrajan. Una vez entré a un bar, el Liquid Beauty Bar, no sé qué. "Get out of here, vieja fea." Así me dicen. Si quiere Dios, vendo todas las flores esa noche y vuelvo a la casa como las diez, once. Si vendo todos mis ramos, me voy ganando como sesenta dólares al día. Que está bien, para una mujer sóla como yo. Pero me está costando, viera. Mis lágrimas y sudor han caído sobre estas calles.

Jim 1: I say, take on the mayor, the board of supervisors.

Jim 2: Let's make them accountable!

Jim 1: We should be cutting deals. Fuck, the biggest economic opportunity since Safeway to hit the Mission in thirty fucking years and we don't want it!?

Jim 2: The internet business moves at light speed. Their economy moves so fast that within a year they will move somewhere else. Meanwhile, we'll still be fighting each other, the dot.com-ers will have gone, and Asian interests will have bought up the Mission once again, because we were so busy killing each other.

Jim 1: ¡Chinos cabrones!

Flower Lady: Bueno, me tengo que ir. Tengo una cita con el doctor de los pies. Como camino tanto, me duelen los "güanates."

(The Jims hang up and see each other face to face.)

Jim 2: Jim!

Jim 1: Vato!

Jim 2: Are you going to the anti-gentrification mixer tonight?

Jim 1: You bet. Where's it at?

Jim 2: Foreign Cinema Restaurant on Mission Street.

Jim 1: See you there.

(The Jims exit. Meanwhile, the Flower Lady has changed into a Cuban transsexual health-care worker, Adelita.)

Adelita: When I was a transvestite and prostitute my name was Hilda. But now that I'm a "straight woman," I changed my name to Adelita. That was the name they gave the women who fought with Pancho Villa, tu sabes. They would cook, they would clean, they would fuck, I love that! That's who I am. When I came from Cuba to San Francisco, I got my first culture shock. I met other Latinas, but they didn't speak the way that I do, they didn't dance the way that I do, they didn't fuck the way that I do. So, I had to learn to be un poquito más Mexicana, un poquito más Salvadoreña, then I was accepted. But now I really like it. I really like Chicano culture. I like what happens to people that are brought to America. I like the confusion! It makes it very . . . anything goes! ¿Tu sabes? And, I'm that way by nature.

I'm a health educator now, and I work with transgender clients, prostitutes, drug users, because there is a lot of drugs in the Mission. But, mainly, it's white kids. They came from Colorado, I don't know why.

On Saturdays, I have a group with straight Latinas. And we engage in conversations about dicks, lovers and fucking and all this, and most of the time their husbands or lovers, they go to jail. And I know a lot of queens that love to go to jail because they can get these mens to pay attention to them. And these mens just want sex, tu sabes? And some of these queens are HIV-positive. So when these mens get out of jail, they have their wives and kids waiting for them. And the wife can't mention condoms to him because he will think that she has been fucking around while he was in jail! So we have a lot of Latinas that are HIV-positive and nobody talks about it. We have bisexuality in the barrio and nobody talks about it. We have transgender issues in our community and nobody talks about. Check this out honeys.

(Adelita snaps her fingers and a cha-cha song is heard. Lights change and a Doctor in a white lab coat enters holding a clipboard.)

Doctor: The Transgender Umbrella was created to identify gender-identity disorders. First, we have the Cross-dresser or Drag—cross-dressing for political or social activism ("queer pride"), humor and/or entertainment.

(An actor wearing a dress and wig enters and then exits.)

Next, wearing articles of clothing associated with the other sex for erotic purposes, is the Transvestite Fetishist.

(The same actor wearing women's lingerie and whip enters and then exits.)

Wow! A transgenderist is someone in transition to become a transsexual; living in gender congruent with gender-identity to resolve gender-identity conflicts. ¡Adelita!

(Adelita turns and dances.)

And, finally, we have the full woman!

(A female stagehand wearing a headset reluctantly enters, gives the Doctor the finger and stomps off.)

Curb your enthusiasm, young lady. Fucking hetero! And that is the Transgender Umbrella. I am Dr. _____. Thank you.

(The Doctor exits. Adelita comes downstage and addresses the audience:)

Adelita: The Transgender Umbrella was formed to unite the different groups. But, the problem with the Umbrella is that there is envy between the different categories. For example, *(To female audience member)* "I have titties, and you don't, bitch." You know what I'm saying? Así está la cosa. That's the way it is. I've moved up the ladder, I'm now a transsexual motivated to surgery, meaning in two years I have my pussy. Then I will be complete. But that's after hormones, steroids, therapy, toda esa onda. Oh, after that, you end up so tired, you just want to spend a week on the Russian River!

My transition started in 1995. And it's a very long process. I had to go to therapy, because I kept considering myself a

gay man. So, when I started living with my boyfriend who is straight, he had a problem that I was still a gay man. But, what do you want me to tell you, that I don't like my dick to be touched? Yes. It's my sexual organ, tú sabes. So, when I first got together with my boyfriend, we never addressed the dick—my dick. I got really tired, because I didn't come when I was getting fucked. So, I would have to whack it afterwards, tú sabes? So I said, "What's up with this?" But we discussed it.

(Adelita's Lover enters. He is a Mexican cowboy wearing a mustache, hat, boots and thong underwear.)

Lover: Adela, you know I've never touched a penis before, but I'm in love with you, vieja. So, I'll do it, if that's going to make you happy. Orale!

(The Lover exits.)

Adelita: So, that was cool! Wow! ¿Es un papi chulo verdad? ¡Muy Tigre del Norte! OK, let's say when I become a woman, I marry him, I have my pussy, knock on wood. We move away from my community to a quiet little town, like Orinda and we adopt and raise kids, I become like Martha Stewart. Oh, but honey, I don't see myself in the PTA meetings! You know what I mean? ¡Porque yo soy medio loca, tú sabes!

Now a lot of people want to know what will happen to my dick. Depends on where you go. If you go to Tijuana, you get a four-thousand-dollar pussy. They cut it off, they make a hole and that's it. You just have a hole. But my operation is going to cost fifty thousand dollars. It's going to be in Colorado. I don't know why. And if you're uncut, like I am, it's great because you have all this skin to work with. Basically what they do is cut the dick in four parts and put it back inside your cavity and the skin of your dick becomes the lining of your pussy. And the head of your dick becomes your clitoris. The skin of your balls, tu sabes, el escroto, becomes your lips. It's very good-looking. And if you do it here, in the United States, you can always go back for a touch-up. I just love America!

(Movie Lady, an old lady wearing a thick wool coat and carrying a shopping bag enters. She sits down and feeds the pigeons.)

Movie Lady: There are a lot of good people around but not like before. It was wonderful in the Mission. You didn't have to lock your doors. You could walk home at ten, eleven o'clock at night and nobody would bother you. Or you could take the streetcar up and down 24th. We'd walk to Mission Street and to all the movie palaces—the Grand, the Crown, the New Mission, 7-UP bottle cap shows at the El Capitán—or we would see vaudeville shows or dance to the big bands.

(Glen Miller's "Moonlight Serenade" is heard.)

Oh, the El Capitán was so beautiful, so classy. The façade was majestic. Oh, but now it's a parking lot, what a shame. We never had any Orientals or Spanish people here. After World War II, the Europeans moved out to the avenues, and bought homes on the G.I. Bill, and the Spanish people moved into the Mission. There were so many vacancies. My parents used to have a grocery store on the corner of 24th and York—Stelli's Market. A block down from the five-and-dime. I still live on York Street and I've been going to the Saint Francis Ice Cream Parlor for over sixty years, since I was a little girl. My father would always buy me salt-water taffy.

My lord, there was Hale's Department Store, Byron's Shoes, Newberry's, Woolworths, Leeds, where my mother bought our Catholic school uniform shoes, the Ideal, Kress. I remember going to the Roosevelt theater to see *Random Harvest* with Ronald Coleman and Greer Garson, so romantic. And they used to give out free dishes.

(She pulls a plate from her shopping bag.)

Oh yeah! I have the whole collection. I tried to give them to my grandchildren, but nobody wants them. Nobody cares about the old stuff anymore. But I still treasure it.

That's all for you, birdies. Time for my supper. You know the Mormon church, in Bernal Heights, where the Samoans go? Well tonight is all-you-can-eat spaghetti, every Tuesday, I never miss it. I usually take some to go.

One more thing. People here think that I was born in New York because of my accent. But I tell them I got the Mission accent. It's just how I talk. All the old-timers got this accent. I'm not from Brooklyn, honey, I'm from the Mission!

(She gathers her things and exits. "Feelings" is heard. César, a man in a long leather coat enters dancing. He wears a lot of gaudy gold jewelry, a thick gold chain and equally thick accent.)

César: César's Latin Palace was the first salsa club in San Francisco. The first! I had the original César's in North Beach, César's in San José and, of course, César's Latin Dancing in the Mission. I would open Thursday nights, Friday nights, with disco dancing 'til four A.M. Saturdays was for benefits and Sunday afternoon was Filipino tea dancing. *(Sings)* "Peelings, nothing more than peelings . . ." Get it? "Peelings." Así hablan los Filipinos . . .

I had the best orchestras. Everybody played here: Willie Colón, Willie Bobo, Tito Puente, Eddie Palmieri, Celia Cruz, you name it. Santana played here. I know Carlos. I know Chepito, I knew Jerry García. I knew Bill Graham, very well, very well. If there was no Bill Graham, there'd be no Santana. Oh, but the scene with the drugs was very heavy in those days. Grass, you know? I remember Santana had two guys rolling grass. They were smoking two, three hours. Compadre, what's going on? La rumba! So I learned to say: "Pass." "Pass," you know, because I didn't smoke. So when the marijuana cigarette came to me, I would say: "Pass."

San Francisco had many good bands and they all played here. There was Malo, El Sapo, Azteca. Then later, Bata-

changa, Benny Valarde, Salsa Caliente and Alma del
Barrio. Now, that was the Mission sound.

(Alma del Barrio's "San Francisco" is heard. César dances
around. The music suddenly stops.)

But, later, the system tried to knock me down. The Alcohol
and Beverage Commission tried to close me down so many
times. They tried to take away my cabaret license. They
said César was selling beer to minors. César never sold beer
to minors. Never. I got on their black list. So I was forced to
sell "near beer." But I sold real beer. I won! There is always
a way, you know. I call it "El Chi Chi."

I came to San Francisco in 1957, from Bolivia, with
twenty-five cents in my pocket, walking on Market Street.
I was twenty-one. By the time I was thirty years, I was
already a millionaire! I became a millionaire through hard
work and brains.

This morning, there was a blackout in the Mission for
instance. There's a little place on Mission and 25th Street,
owned by Peruvian guys . . .

(Two Peruvian coffee shop owners enter. They speak at the same
time.)

Peruvians: César, we have no coffee.
César: What do you mean, you don't have coffee?
Peruvians: We have no electricity.
César: You don't need electricity to make coffee. Do you have
gas?
Peruvians: Sí.
César: Do you have water?
Peruvians: Sí.
César: You boil water with the gas, put the hot water through the
coffee grinds and you have coffee! That's it!
Peruvians: Oooooohhh. But you are César.
César: No, it's not because I'm César! It's just a simple thing.
Like in Latin America, a tire blowout, you get out and (huff,
puff) you put it back, that's it.

Peruvians: Ooooooohhh. Gracias César.

(The Peruvians exit.)

César: You see, I studied clinical psychology and economics. You use them every day. I never thought I was less than anybody. In the beginning, the Italians in North Beach, they used to call me "El Mexicano." All the time. That never bothered me. They used to say, "How are the tacos? How are the enchiladas?" I used to say, "Great, great." With a smile. So one time, I went to the bank and deposited a quarter of a million dollars. Next day, I was not "El Mexicano," I was "Césare. Bon giorno, Césare."

("Feelings" is heard again. César slow dances, lost in his memories. Music slowly fades out.)

And then, I became a Republican. I went to the White House several times. President Reagan invited me. President Bush. El papá, no el hijo pendejo, W.

I got into city politics because there was nobody to challenge City Hall. There was no respect. So I said, "Someone must tell them we live here, in the Mission." People said, "Oh, César is doing it for the taxes or publicity." But, no. I used my own money. I never asked for money. I'd go out in my fire truck and campaign. The first time, in '84, Mrs. Dianne Feinstein spent 2.8 million dollars in the election. I spent eleven thousand dollars. She beat me by only twenty-five thousand votes.

Many people tell me to run for mayor again. I think I will do. I think I will do. One day, I will be mayor. The first salsa mayor of San Francisco! César for mayor! Viva César!

(Alma del Barrio's "San Francisco" is heard again. César salsa dances offstage.

Music and lights change. Nat King Cole's "Nature Boy" is heard. Jack Wickert, a middle-aged hippie/artist enters.)

Jack Wickert: We moved here in 1943. War came and everybody had to move off their farms. So we left forty acres in Wisconsin to come out west. Father worked in the shipyards, mother worked at Bethlehem Steel.

When we were kids, we used to kick balls up on the roof of Borden's Dairy. My brother, Art Wickert, was the meanest kid on Potrero Hill. In 1951, we moved down to 24th and Bryant. The mustard-colored house around the corner. I was going to Mission High and hanging out at Saint Francis's Malt Shop and Roosevelt's Tamale Parlor.

Mission High, man. Mission High had great spirit and a good football team. We had Garland Blueford, the all-city halfback. He's a preacher now. We had a great band at the Mission Boy's Club, too. And we looked cool man. Powder blue, one button roll. Powder blue, one button roll. We wore black shoes, like the Pachucos see, and guys from Saint Ignatius and Sacred Heart wore white shoes. And if you went to Lowell, you wore brown-and-white saddle loafers with cardigan sweaters. Ouch! In any language. That just ain't right.

I grew up on 24th Street, you know. Oh yeah. There was a riff here and there, but hell, we all ran together. Irish, Mexican, Italian, Polish, German. We were all straight, happy Eisenhower kids. We won the war and we were on top of the world. We were all typical mongrel Americans. See, Dad was German, Mom was French-Polish. Typical mongrel Americans.

The Mission was a very full and happy kind of place. You know what we would do? On Friday nights, we'd drink beer up on the side of Potrero Hill where the old Annex is now. See, back then, kids had places to go and things to do. The politicians changed all that forever. Fucking politicians. Dianne Feinstein. *(Shudders)* She went to Lowell. Bunch of Lowell cherries!

True story. My dog, Hey Pup, bit the shit out of Dianne Feinstein. One day, at the Farm, Feinstein came marching through with her martinet and her little bow-tie and her *Planet of the Apes* hairdo, and that startled poor Hey Pup. And Hey Pup jumped off the couch and grabbed onto

Feinstein's ankle, and wouldn't let go. We were surprised as shit when Feinstein bit the dog back! But Hey Pup was a good dog.

I drove a cab in the city. One night, my cab breaks down at the airport. I'm depressed, college education, what am I gonna do? Just then, I hear an announcement over the radio: "San Francisco Mime Troupe, looking for a trumpet player." I could play trumpet, I could read music, write a score. I got the gig. Tour the Southwest, see the world. Ha ha ha. Luis Valdez and Peter Coyote were gone from the troupe by then, but I met up with Peter later at Black Bear Commune. He used to wear a feather in his hair. Living on a commune, banging two chicks at a time. Well, that's just what Peter does. "Oracle, powering the internet."

Malcolm and Zoe were up there, too. They started the Community Garden. But that's when I laid into them. I said, "You fucking hippies. You come into the Mission, you start all this shit, and then you flee to the communes in the country. Meanwhile, we're stuck here in the city, watching weed and mushrooms turn to speed and heroin." I didn't care for that.

I guess I'm just a populist Mission kid. I remember when Bonnie had some cows near the freeway by the Farm. My name is Jack, and I live in a boathouse here on Mission Creek, at the end of the Stream of Sorrows. And every year, the pile worms return to do their wiggly squiggly in front of my boathouse. And I'm just afraid those six thousand units across the Mission Bay are going to screw that up for the pile worms. That's not nostalgia, folks, that's Mother Nature. Hell, I'm so old, I remember when Bill Irwin had a CETA job!

Before I leave, one more thing. Sal García tells a story about an old Indian named Makuka. He's a homeless cat who lives up in Dolores Park and he wears a talisman around his neck. The tooth of some wild animal. Anyway, one night, Makuka is getting robbed by two young punks, and they say, "Give us all your money, Makuka." And he says, "I don't have any." "Well then, give us that tooth around your neck." And Makuka says, "You want the *tooth*? You can't handle the *tooth*!" Ha ha ha!

(Jack Wickert exits. Lights change. "Barrio Mission" is heard again. Herbert enters followed by a Pachuco, who saunters across the stage.)

Pachuco:
> *Carnal, ese, sabes que*
> don't I know you?
> Didn't we meet
> eyes, una vez
> didn't I kiss your heart
> once? Calmado.
>
> I am sure I know you
> oye carnal
> didn't you
> use to live
> next to me
> a un ladito?
> I remember that if I
> reached out, I could touch you.
>
> It was a long time ago
> then you split
> *querías conocer el mundo*
> te acuerdas?
>
> Simón, I'm sure
> it was you.
> Do you know me carnal?

(Pachuco exits.)

Herbert: Rodrigo Reyes, Chicano, farmworker, high school graduate, licenciado, taxi driver, enamorado, activista encabronado, escritor, pinto, a veces actor y director, amante de hombres y mujeres y el mundo.

I remember the first time I met Rodrigo, it was back in '77. I had just graduated from Balboa High and I was now a hippie art student from CCAC. I was delivering some La

Raza silkscreen posters to the Capp Street Neighborhood Center where Rodrigo was director.

(Video image of Rodrigo Reyes is seen.)

He was a tall, dark, handsome Tejano with a thick mustache and a full head of salt-and-pepper. He had classic good looks. Like film star Pedro Armendáriz. He had a deep resonant broadcasting voice that boomed, Atención! Even though he was impressive, he had a peculiar gentle lazy Texan walk . . . like he was walking backwards. I was eighteen. He sized me up and down.

(Rodrigo enters.)

Rodrigo: How would you like to be in a play? I'm forming an all-Spanish-speaking theater company for the people of the Mission.
Herbert: Since I knew Spanish, and wanted to be John Travolta, I joined his company.
Rodrigo: Welcome to Teatro Gusto!

(The men shake hands.)

Herbert: We held general auditions for our first play, the Mexican classic, *Los Desarraigados: The Uprooted.* They were awful. We basically hired people who could speak Spanish, but not necessarily act. Rodrigo had us go through all the basic theater exercises.
Rodrigo: The mirror exercise!

(The two men mirror each other.)

Animales!

(The two men get down on their knees and growl and bark like dogs.)

Group massage!

(Rodrigo starts massaging Herbert's back. It starts getting erotic. Herbert breaks away.)

Herbert: We premiered at the Mission Cultural Center. And from the first night, we were hooked. We went out celebrating on our opening night, like we had just conquered Broadway or something. We would go to La Rondalla, a Mexican restaurant that is decorated like Christmas all year round. Some nights, Rodrigo would take me to Esta Noche Nightclub. And we would get very drunk, stumble out into the streets and sing old Bee Gee songs all the way to his flat on Guerrero Street.

One night, Rodrigo invited me over to his place to have dinner. When I came in, I noticed that candles were lit, giant sunflowers were in vases. His apartment was immaculate. The perfect color-coordinated serape on the couch, the ubiquitous Virgin de Guadalupe. And, of course, the famous Diego Rivera print. I sat on the couch, and he put on some Juan Gabriel music!

("Querida" by Juan Gabriel is heard.)

After a delicious meal of pollo con canela, Rodrigo says to me:

Rodrigo: You know, Herbert, I'm gay . . . would you like some flan?

Herbert: Rodrigo had become my best friend. I left for Los Angeles in 1990 and lost touch with Rodrigo. On one of my visits to the Mission, I saw him sitting at the bar of La India Bonita.

(An old Pedro Infante song is heard.)

I tapped on the window. He waved me to come in and we had a beer together. I told him I had just taped a pilot sitcom in Hollywood. He said he was organizing drag queens and producing shows at the Victoria Theater. Then, he said to me:

Rodrigo: You know, Herbert, I'm HIV-positive. Would you like another cerveza?

(Rodrigo exits.)

Herbert: Rodrigo looked great. His spirits were high, and he was working and educating his community he loved so much—the Mission. This is a man who knew all the risks, yet, perhaps to him, death was a kind of aphrodisiac.

(Pachuco enters.)

Pachuco:
>Aquí entre nos
>la muerte no es
>una calavera,
>sino una preciosa
>calaca.
>
>No es un ser
>como dicen, del mas allá
>esta aquí entre nosotros
>vivita y culeando.
>
>Aquí entre nos
>vida, pasión y muerte
>son más que un bonito título
>sino una estupefaciente
>realidad.
>
>No, la muerte no es
>una calavera, sino una
>preciosa calaca.
>
>Ahora se cubre de besos
>de un mortal menage a trois.

Herbert: I went back to Hollywood and made my self even busier. I felt helpless and in denial that he would ever get sick. But, sure enough, a friend of ours called me and said Rodrigo had been hospitalized and had been very sick, but was now back home. I immediately flew up to see him. He was now living on San José Avenue, across the hall from my friend René Yañez. I walked into his bright airy room. The whole room was white with only five lit veladoras. Rodrigo had set the stage for la muerte's grand entrance.

(Rodrigo enters looking weak and wearing a robe.)

Rodrigo: Por poco me voy muriendo, I almost died. But, Herbert, I'm going to beat this.

Herbert: Dementia and the morphine were talking. I told him that I had a videotape of a sitcom pilot that I wanted to show him.

Rodrigo: Well, pop it in while I go take a piss. These medicinas really make me piss alot. Go ahead, Herbert. I'm going to call Juan Pablo. Pop it in, Herbert, you're at home.

Herbert: He slowly got out of bed and went towards the bathroom. I was shocked to see how skinny, how frail he had become. Like an old man or child.

He came back and laid back down, grunting and groaning. I played him the tape. He looked proud as the beginning credits rolled. This was the young man he had recruited to do "teatro," and now he was doing sitcoms in Hollywood. After the show was over, he said:

Rodrigo: You know, Herbert, that was real shitty.

(Rodrigo slowly exits.)

Herbert: It was shitty. Rodrigo dozed in and out. Finally, I think my visit wore him out. I sat by his bedside, kissed him on the forehead, and left. The room was bright white. That afternoon, I walked the streets of the sunny Mission, remembering how Rodrigo would also enjoy strolling those same streets in his lazy, casual, Texan walk.

(Pachuco enters. Carlos Santana music underscores.)

Pachuco: ¿Carnal, ese, sabes que? Don't I know you? Didn't we meet eyes, una vez? Didn't I kiss your heart once? Calmado.

(Pachuco exits.)

Herbert: Two weeks later, I got a call that Rodrigo had died. But he's not gone, he's here, among us, walking in the Mission.

(Herbert exits. Jerry García's "Walking in the Rain" is heard. Video image of people walking in the Mission is projected. Two activists enter as video and music fade.)

Ronnie Burke: All my friends who bought into AZT early on, died horrible deaths. Okay? You have to understand that, alright? AZT, ddI, ddC, d4T, 3TC, ILS, Crixivan, Sustiva, these are the worst, *the worst*, drugs possible for immuno-suppression. Big pharmaceutical companies are making hundreds of millions of dollars off AIDS, AIDS research and AIDS hysteria. And that's why we say, "AIDS is over!"

ACT UP Critic: I'm able to sit here and talk to you because of the prescription drugs I take. ACT UP/San Francisco is dangerous and out of control They are nothing more than a small group of people who are able to leverage their wealth from millions of dollars in sales of medical marijuana and spread their dissident message that AIDS is over. That's bullshit and it's irresponsible.

Ronnie Burke: I'm able to sit here and talk to you because of the drugs I do *not* take. We only enshrine dead fags. Nobody cares about fags living with HIV. I actually went to the AIDS Foundation for help, and they put me in the Mission Hotel. Let me tell you, the building is not suitable for living. It's infested with rats, lice and roaches. So I did some research and I found that workers at the AIDS Foundation had tried to organize to raise their wages. Some organizers had been beaten up and fired. Spanish is not allowed to be spoken in the office. Now that's real outreach to the Mission. So I threw cat shit on Pat Christen, the executive director of San Francisco AIDS Foundation, the AIDS czar of the city who makes one hundred and seventy-five dollars a year. The President of the United States makes two hundred dollars . . . blah blah blah.

ACT UP Critic: Todd Swindell, David Pasquarelli, Michael Bellefountaine and Ronnie Burke have pissed off so many people that there are forces rising up to bring them down. ACT UP/San Francisco is violent. They spit, they throw things . . . they're gross!

Ronnie Burke: Duh. This is what happened. I went to a meeting where Pat Christen and some other "AIDS experts" were talking to the community. I had this big bag of dirty kitty litter, and I'm making my way towards her, and let me tell you, Pat Christen is a lot bigger than I am. She's a lady who goes to the gym, I guess, I mean the bitch was strong. I'm just a little, skinny Mexican guy. Anyway, I'm arm wrestling with Pat and the cops throw me against the wall, and the cat shit goes flying everywhere, and it doesn't even hit her. When I got to the police station, they were asking me what was that? "Dirty kitty litter," I told them. And they said, "Well, one of our cops is sick." "Well, he better take a shower," I said. And they said, "Why did you do that?" And I said, "Because it's the end of the millennium and I intend on having fun."

ACT UP Critic: Ronny Burke is insane. ACT UP/SF is outcast.

Ronnie Burke: After the attack, I was pleased, because Pat Christen came to light. And she is now the most hated public figure in the city.

ACT UP Critic: What a crock. She's done a fabulous job. ACT UP/SF are terrorists. And please, don't buy pot from their Cannabis Club!

(ACT UP Critic exits.)

Ronnie Burke: Bye. Well, you can see what pharmaceuticals are doing for his sunny disposition. After the attack, I was very angry. But, in the end, I had to do twenty-four hours of community service at Galería de la Raza, in the Mission. It was really "hard work." *(Wink)* It turned out to be an hour for each pound of cat shit. Bye.

(Ronnie Burke exits. A Gay Activist storms in.)

Gay Activist: I want you to pie Robin Williams! The next time you see him in the Castro, just pie his ass! I heard he wants to play Harvey Milk in the Harvey Milk movie. Come fucking on! You mean Hollywood can't find one New York Jewish fag actor to play that fag? Come on people! They're going to get Mork, "Nanoo Nanoo," to play Harvey? Fuck you!!!

(Gay Activist exits. A big Black Woman enters.)

Black Woman: Mayor Willie Brown is a very, very nice man. I know, I make his hats. He has given me a lot of good advice on account of I'm considered the "Mayor of the Fillmore." He's a very intelligent man, but I just stay outta the man's way. Last year, he got his with a cherry pie in the head. I thought it was stupid for them to do that. Folks were calling it a racist attack. I don't think there was nothing racist about it, I mean they throw pies at anybody. My minister wanted everybody to go over and protest. I ain't gonna do that shit. Because those people are crazy, that's just what they do. They threw pies at Bill Gates, now you can't get no whiter than Mr. Microsoft! But let me tell you somethin', if anybody throws a pie at my face, I'm gonna kick their ass!

(Black Woman exits. Dylan, an Irish bar patron enters.)

Dylan: How dare they throw a pie at the mayor. Jesus, Mary and Joseph, give me a fucking break! The mayor's been so damned good to us Irish. Everybody in this bar voted for him. *(Offstage voices shout assent)* I dare you to walk into Clooney's and throw a shepherd's pie in me face. I'll kick the shit outta ya! *(Offstage voices shout threats)*

(Dylan exits. A Latino Evangelist enters with a bull horn).

Evangelist: Hallelujah! Hallelujah! Sálvanos. Cherry pie! Cherry pie! Cristo! Sálvanos. Cherry García. Cherry García. Wavy Gravy . . . ¡Jesú Cristo!

(A Salvadorean enters.)

Salvadorean: ¡Calláte cerote! ¡Evangélico hijo de puta! Andá gritá por otra parte, cerote!

(Evangelist exits).

¡Miren, me vale verga Willie Brown y cherry pies! ¡Lo que me ostiga a mi es que ya ni una pupusa se puede comer en la Misión, vaya! ¡Hay comida Vietnamesa, comida Irlandesa, comida Francesa, comida Japonesa, hasta comida Marueca! ¡Pero pupusas, ya no hay, por la gran puta!

(Salvadorean exits. A bionic Pie Thrower activist storms in.)

Pie Thrower: We pied Willie Brown with a cherry pie, probably not a good idea. The mayor thought that his head had exploded. You are aware that a mayor was killed in San Francisco?

Alright, the pieing was during a press conference for the new 49ers stadium. Another multimillion dollar project the mayor's cronies are doing. Burger King was sponsoring the whole event. They were ready to put this gold paper crown on the mayor's head and he said, "And now for something very dramatic." And that's when Justin comes up from the left and says, "Matrix this!" That's the leftover economic plan from former Mayor Jordan. Then, a bunch of goons jump on Justin, and the mayor steps back from the podium, wiping the cherry pie from his face. And, as soon as he opens his eyes, I come up and get him with the coup de grâce. Noooooooooo. It was beautiful, man!

Now, if you watch the videotape of the pieing, you see the mayor say something like, "Motherfucker this," and, "Motherfucker that." He physically attacks us! I mean, he's getting all ghetto and shit. Then his goons break our partner's shoulder. She's only a hundred and ten pounds, OK. Then, he realizes the cameras are on him and he tries to act all normal and stuff. But, for those few seconds, the *true evil* that is Willie Brown comes out!

So, in all the chaos, the cops are trying to gather the pie evidence and there's this little mascot pig, probably from Schwartz Sausage or someplace. Anyway, this pig is eating all the pie fragments, so all the cops could do was to collect the pie tins and put them into "evidence bags."

It was not an attack on *Mr.* Brown, it was a statement on *Mayor* Brown's policies. So, I did some time, six weeks thank you very much! The sheriffs were like, "Good job. Can I get your autograph?"

You have to have a pie and a vision to work at the Bionic Bakery. And if you want to take up pie throwing, remember: always shoot for the upper crust.

(Pie Thrower exits. Jefferson Airplane's "White Rabbit" is heard. Two middle-aged hippie women enter. They place their stools center stage. White Maria rolls a joint. Latina Betita drinks wine from a glass.)

Maria: I'm trying to raise my daughter with awareness. She begged me for a Barbie doll, so I bought her the frickin' Barbie under one condition: that she'd be an Activist Barbie.

Betita: Right on!

Maria: A Barbie with a conscience. And, I didn't like how Barbie looked anatomically either, you know, too perfect. So, to my daughter's dismay, I took a pen and drew in her armpit and pubic hairs. What can I say, I'm a product of the '60s. How's the wine? It's Chilean.

Betita: Fabulous.

Maria: I have tea honey. ¿Yerba mate?

Betita: No, really, the wine is divine. So, does little Rigoberta still go to César Chávez Elementary?

Maria: Of course. I love it, it's so progressive. You know, it might be the only school in the country that sends parent permission slips home with the children addressed to "the collective." The third graders organized a trip to Kandahar. All the parents are involved in grassroots organizing and stuff. You know me, I love that. You have to be a revolutionary to be my friend.

Betita: Sometimes, I feel like we are the last ones left in the Mission. That's why I had to leave Fresno, too damn conservative.

Maria: Ooh, Fresno's gross. I thought you were from Corpus Christi?

Betita: No, that was Amalia, mujer.

Maria: Seems like a whole army of mujeres came from Texas.

Betita: I came to the Mission and wanted to join the Black Panther Party, but I wasn't allowed so instead I joined the Pickle Family Circus.

Maria: The Mission's got soul! Oh, my god, I'm getting a flashback.

Betita: ¿Cuidado con los hot flashes?

Maria: No, honey. Not a hot flash, a flashback. I'm not *that* fucking vieja. I'm remembering at Mission High, you were either a surfer or a soul. They would come right up to you: "What are you a surfer or a soul?"

Betita: What were you?

Maria: I thought I was a soul. I wanted to be Angela Davis, but with my blond hair, I looked more like Wavy Gravy. You want a super-charge?

Betita: Indeed.

(Maria gives Betita a super-charge.)

Head rush. Where did you get the grass?

Maria: My nephew. He goes to Berkeley High. He just got a scholarship to go to Humbolt State.

Betita: I remember I wanted to be a Chicana Gloria Steinem, and put all those macho Chicanos in their place. And some on their backs. The Mission brings out the proletariat in you. I came to the Mission to agitate, and never left. Where else can you agitate and double-park your car for an hour?

Maria: One time, I didn't have registration or tags on my car for five years. And I never got caught.

Betita: Good for you.

Marla: I'm just a white Mission ghetto person.

Betita: La Gringita de la Misión.

Maria: La *Güera* de la Misión. I prefer "Güera." But you know, I always got shit from the women of color. And I never understood that. Look, I've lived in the Mission most of my life. I volunteered for the trial of Los Siete. I helped move and sell arms for El Salvador, Nicaragua, Chile, the IRA and I have lived through eleven dictatorships at the Mission Cultural Center. And I'm tired of apologizing for who I am. I've been here longer than most people. I got it from the black women when I dated Jamal.

Betita: I remember him. The drummer from Dolores Park, with the dreadlocks.

Maria: That's right. He looked like Mumia. Then, I got it from the Latinas when I dated Esteban. You remember him, he looked like Che. Now, I get it from the new generation of Latinas. I was at San Francisco State the other day, and I'm getting attitude and stares at the Chiapas and utility protest. So this Chicana-Mechista is looking at me like I don't belong. And I know this girl, her name is Tonantzín, it used to be Tiffany. Her little matching huipil from the Urban Outfitter didn't fool me. I was talking to Guillermo Gómez-Peña the other night at a wild loft party.

Betita: He's gorgeous.

Maria: And I say to Guillermo, "I am seeing something new in the Mission, and it's something I have seen growing. The escalation of brown on brown crime. Not just the north/south gang thing, but also Yucatecos and Central Americans killing each other, fighting the cops. This is not winning in the court of popular opinion." I have yet to see a gang of dot.com kids surround a Latino kid and kick his butt. And Guillermo says that, "The brown on brown violence is systematic of the economic and social pressure pushing down on the Mission right now. The money, the squeezing of space, and this pressure plays itself out, sometimes violently on the streets." He is so smart.

Betita: You never read about that.

Maria: It's a black out, is what it is.

Betita: Well, I was on Valencia the other day.

Maria: ¿Baja Noe?

Betita: Uh-huh. And I saw a terrible fight, in front of the Slanted Door.

Maria: Norteño and Sureños gang kids?

Betita: No. Two yuppies, fighting for the last table.

Maria: They were probably from No Mo.

Betita: No Mo?

Maria: "No Mo Mexicans Live Here."

(The two women laugh.)

Betita: That's terrible.

Maria: That's fucked-up, and you shouldn't be laughing.

Betita: It's terribly shameful what's happening to the artists in the Mission.

Maria: Shameful is the word.

Betita: René and Yolanda will probably have to move.

Maria: No . . .

Betita: They're being evicted.

Maria: No . . .

Betita: They've lived forever in that house.

Maria: I know!

Betita: Rio was born in that house.

Maria: I know!

Betita: Rodrigo died in that house.

Maria: I know. Well, they're gonna have to drag me outta here, too. Because I am fighting to the death. An arts community with no artists. Sometimes, I get so angry, that I want to yell at the mayor to suck my dick! *(Pause)* I've got to mellow out. I don't have a dick. The Mission is changing too fucking fast. With René and the other artists moving out, the Mission's lost its soul, and there's no turning back.

Betita: The other day, I was driving, going west on 16th Street, and I wanted to make a left turn, and I did a sort of bad thing. OK, well, actually, I made a left turn from the far right lane and I clipped this big SUV, very slightly. I mean we barely hit each other. So we both pulled over into the bus stop on 16th Street. I get out of my car and the woman driving doesn't want to come out. She doesn't even roll down the window! She stays sitting in her car, high up. I say I'm sorry, 'cause it was my fault. And then, she starts talking to me. Through a microphone!

Maria: A microphone?

Betita: A microphone. *(Nasal voice)* "Do you have insurance?" *(Normal)* The whole street can hear this woman! She wouldn't roll down her window! She was terrified of me. She was terrified of being on 16th and Mission. By now, there is a crowd of people. All these broken-down folks start getting involved. They didn't like how she was talking down to me. The people on 16th started to surround her car. *(Nasal voice)* "Everybody stand back! I have called the police!" *(Normal)* So, the homeless people start coming up to me and say, "I saw it, sister, I saw. It was *her* fault!" This other guy, who could hardly walk, comes up to me and says, "I'll be your witness, lady. *She* hit *you*." Everybody started chanting: "You're right. She's wrong. You're right. She's wrong." All these poor broken-down folk yelling. They were so mad at her for talking down to me. Some even started to shake her car! Well, she freaked-out and sped out of the bus stop. Then everybody around me cheered. And, well, this really made my day. You can never underestimate the power of the people of the Mission.

Maria: El pueblo unido, jamás será vencido.

Maria and Betita: ¡El pueblo unido, jamás será vencido!

Betita: Shit happens in the Mission.

Maria: I love the "Missh." I just don't know how long I can afford to stay here.

Betita: I love my 24th Street.

Maria: I love Galería de la Raza.

Betita: I love Balmy Alley.

Maria: I love all the murals.

Betita: I love Precita Park.

Maria: I love Carnaval.

Betita: I love Frutilandia

Maria: I love Dolores Park.

Betita: I love Mitchell's mango ice cream.

Maria: I love Discolandia. You know, Berta? I love Culture Clash. Richard is sexy.

Betita: Ric's got cute buns.

Maria: And Herbert? He's . . . *(Pause)* . . . bald.

Betita: I love the San Francisco Mime Troupe.

(Fact Wino, a San Francisco Mime Troupe character enters and leaves. The ladies turn around, they think they saw something.)

Maria: We love Carlos Santana.

(The ladies turn around but Carlos Santana never appears.)

Betita: Oooh. I think I have the munchies.

Maria: King's Bakery.

Betita: Trilingual Asians, who sell pan dulce.

Maria: Three Chinese brothers. I dated the one who looks like Mao.

Betita: Burritos?

Maria and Betita: ¡¡La Cumbre!!

Maria: Number fifty-four, your carne asade is ready! I love it when they sing out like that. It's just like poetry. I love you. *(Pause)* You know something Betita, I always wanted to marry one of those Chileans from Berkeley . . . *(Long pause)* Jeez, where the hell did that come from?

(The women laugh. They are now very stoned.)

Betita: You know something? I think we're the last of the Red Hot Revolutionaries.

Maria: You want another super-charge?

(They move closer together as the lights fade. "La Mujer Está con la Revolución" by Carlos Puebla is heard. Then an audio testimony is heard:)

Olga: Uh, hi, my name is Olga and I used to live in the Mission. I got evicted, like, two years ago and two years ago, they told us we could move back after one year, but it's already been two. And, they recently just told us that we can only go back for five years, it's a five-year contract. Then, after that, they will be evicting us again and we will no longer be able to live there. When I was evicted from the Army Street Projects, we were moved to Bay View District. After I moved to Bay View, I didn't feel that I was a part of the Mission, I really felt sad, because I was born and raised in the Mission. So I, uh, come here a lot, but it's not the same. I just really want to move back and hopefully I can and, uh, find an affordable place to live in.

(Woody Guthrie's "Pretty Boy Floyd" is heard. Three dot.com slackers enter riding Razor scooters.)

Dotter 1: Hey, Wally, let's go party!

Wally: I can't right now, I'm doing an interview with Culture Clash.

Dotter 2: Fuck them! We're partying at Bruno's!

Dotter 1: C'mon, tonight's "Jungle Vibe"!

Dotter 2: No, it's not! It's "Hip-Hop Vibe."

Wally: I thought it was "Reggae Vibe."

Dotter 1: It's any fucking vibe we wanna buy!

Dotter 2: Hey, let's meet at Blondie's. It's two-for-one apple martinis!

Dotter 1 and 2: S.Y.T.

Wally: See you there.

(Two dot.com slackers exit.)

We're the new economy. You've heard of the "dot.com invasion" and the displacement in the neighborhood. Well, it's not my fault! The worst thing is being hated by people that don't know anything about you. Their methods are way off. The tires of my SUV vehicle have been slashed and my work loft-space has been vandalized and tagged many times. So, living here isn't all that pleasant. I'm here because the square footage is cheaper than downtown. Listen, real estate is astronomical. Blame the greedy developers and tell the city to build low-income housing for families and artists. Don't make me the whipping boy for all the problems in the Mission. I got my own problems. I've exceeded my "burn rate" and I had to lay off six people.

I'm just hoping to hang on or get flipped by a bigger company. If not, I might have to move back to Colorado.

(Wally exits. Omar Sosa piano music is heard. Don Bajema enters with a letter in his hands.)

Don Bajema: If you wanna tell the story . . . I'm okay with whatever you want to do. So I am sending you and the guys this letter:

"I found the coyote the day before Eva died. I was on my way home from doing a movie in L.A. I remember the radio was playing nonstop Dylan, because it was his fiftieth birthday. We were all hoping she'd have a liver transplant to save her. One was found. But then, the doctors came in pretty late that night and said they couldn't perform the surgery. Eva was already too far gone. It was pretty terrible. So, I took Ramona, my daughter, and Jane, my wife, home that morning around dawn, and kept driving up to Mount Tam to bury the coyote. I think Eva García passed that day.

I just couldn't leave that beautiful symbol of California beside the road like that, not when a true daughter of California was dying. I excused myself when I started to disturb the coyote. He was large. In the prime of life, with a bright silver coat. I told the coyote that I couldn't leave him there, and that I had a friend dying, and that I'd bury him on a mountainside, instead of letting him remain by the side of the road."

(Video image of Eva García fades in and out.)

"The whole thing was surreal. Very painful. I think about Eva a lot. Sal and I bring her back in conversations pretty frequently. René and I cried very hard at her funeral. Just tell them, she was a great artist, a beautiful Chicana, and she loved the Mission with all her heart.

She was a big loss to so many people. Especially my daughter Ramona.

—Don Bajema, the Mission, San Francisco."

(Don Bajema exits as lights fade to black. Smokey Robinson's "Cruising" is heard. A Veterano cholo enters.)

Veterano: The first lowrider I ever saw, was in 1976. A blue pearl, two-door, hardtop, '63 Chevy Impala with 14 x 7-inch True Spoke rims and hydraulics. It cruised pass me on 24th and Mission, and I said, "What the fuck was that?" See, you never saw any lowriders in the Mission before, or in San Francisco, for that matter. All you saw was hotrods, *American Graffiti* shit, and mostly white boys, too. And we said chale with that noise. And we got our ranflas, we chopped the springs, we added hydraulics, cherry paint job, booming sound system, and we cruised all night long. Low and slow, even on the freeways! I mean cruising was a way of life. It was like our religion. Mi vida loca. And I'm not talking about that puto, Ricky Martin! And, in its heyday, cruising in the Mission was the place to go. I mean, it was bumper-to-bumper every Friday and Saturday night.

(Old school funk medly is heard. Veterano dances slow cholo-like, then performs some "lock" moves, and becomes young again.)

Hey, Chivo, you got any juice in that ranfla? Well, hop your ride, ese! Orale.

Whassup, homegirl? I'll give you a call. We'll go dancing at the Black Angus. Be by the phone.

Hey, homey, be cool. It's la placa. It's la jura. It's la chota. *(Exasperated)* The police!

Everybody was on the street. It was like the Zócalos of Mexico or Latin America. It was happening on Mission Street. The cholitos were checking out the cars like it was a parade. And it was—a parade of custom-style lowriders. Chevys and Oldsmobiles, pickups and even lowrider Volkswagens. There were car clubs like Brown Pride, Low Conspiracy, Lifestyle, the Crusaders. Now these vatos were serious about their cars. They put a lot of money into their cars. So they didn't want any hassles. Especially from the pigs.

I would pack my ride with my homeboys and cruise up

and down Mission. We weren't saints, but there was no Norteños or Sureños, no red or blue. None of that bullshit. We were out just to have fun, and we'd be drinking Old English 800 and Mickey Big Mouths, toking on some big ol' Cheech and Chong joints, shouting out the window: "Mira, Mami, ven páca. Take a ride in my Impala." And we'd be listening to Santana, War, Tower of Power and oldies all night long.

(Malo's "Suavecito" is heard.)

That song right there is the Chicano National Anthem. A lot of babies were born cuz of that song. And I would hook up with some fine-ass cholitas, especially the ones from Daly City. There was La Joker, Cookie, Blinky, Daisy, Lil Loca, oh yeah, there was also La Frog Face, but there was no one like my baby doll, my main ruca, La Squeaky.

Squeaky *(Voice-over)*: Wassup, Veterano. You looking hella fine, and shit. Hey pick me up later, we'll go dancing okay? Ooh, you lookin' hella fine and shit. Hey Veterano, what's that bitch in the front row looking at? I'll kick her ass, even though I'm pregnant and shit. I love you hella lots Veterano.

Veterano: It's not mine. Hey, La Squeaky would give me some big ol' hickeys. She was the original Chupacabra! After cruising we would go dancing at La Fuente on the Embarcadero, California Hall, Jack Tar Hotel, Obrero Hall, Saint Paul's, or you would just end up cruising back and forth all night long, and finally get a bite at Paco's Taco.

But then it all came to an end. With all the bumper-to-bumper action on Mission Street, it would take Muni buses one whole hour to get from 25th Street to 26th. And with all those Cholitos loitering, littering and vandalizing, the store merchants started to complain. And that's when Mayor Dianne Frankenstein went to war with the lowriders. She sent out the pigs, and they started to harass and ticket us, putting up NO LEFT TURN signs. Those signs are still there. And wooden horses to divert traffic. Shortly after, lowriding in the Mission came to a crashing halt.

(Veterano starts to rap.)

I'm a disciple of the barrio cruising down the street
I see homies copping poses on the hot concrete
An urban jungle hieroglyphics on the wall
My metallic shark swerves and starts to stall
There's no more cruising on the strip, that's all
We got direct orders from City Hall
As the petrol flows and pumps through my veins
My heart stampedes and I can't contain

That I'm a lowrider for life from the days gone by
A Mission homeboy 'til the day I die.

¡Por vida, La Misión forever, y que! Con safos. Shaaaa.

*(Veterano exits. Lights change. A video image of an eye is seen.
Arabic music is heard. Jack Wickert enters.)*

Jack: My friend Sal García tells a story about Makuka and the
phantom Muni bus driver. This Muni bus driver has been
dead a long time. But he still drives his route—the 14
Mission.

(The Muni Bus Driver crosses the stage and exits.)

This bus driver's been known to kill his passengers by running them over and over again. The phantom Muni bus
driver takes the same route that the old gondolas did when
they navigated down the Stream of Sorrows. If you see this
phantom bus parked out in front of the Magic Donut Shop
on 20th and Mission, around three in the morning: do not
get on the fucking bus! Once you get on, you will never get
off.
  Some people swear they see Jerry García on the phantom bus with the Brown Buffalo, Saint Francis of Assisi, still
bleeding from stigmatas, dead cholos on PCP, dead cops,
Costanoan Indians, white kids from the Midwest who die of
heroin overdoses in Mission District doorways, trouba-
dours who sing sad songs and middle-aged Central American women who sell dead roses.

*(Fog horns and a stream of water is heard. The Flower Lady
enters. She sits down center stage.)*

Where the wild violets grew in profusion
the day was Friday
Friday of Sorrows

Our Lady of Sorrows Lagoon begins at Mission Dolores. That's why the exploitive Spanish built the Mission there in the first place. Fresh water. The Stream of Sorrows flowed beneath the Mission.

(A Gondolier with a paddle crosses the stage and exits.)

I've seen old lithographs of men paddling their gondolas near 16th and Harrison, then slowly moving across Treat Street. A river has always run through her.

> Arroyo de Nuestra Senora del los Dolores
> Serpentine Creek
> Precita Creek
> Islas Creek

These were abundant fishing places for eons. Long before the conquistadores came. The Alonian and Costanoan Indians were skilled fishermen. Anchovies, mackerels, shiners, muscles, striped bass . . .

(A video image of roses is seen.)

The stream flows in front of the boathouses and the 3rd Street Bridge near McCovey Cove.

> She is the River
> a place of contradiction,
> copulation,
> mystery and
> magic
> and the occasional
> miracle
> micas
> micas
> to all our relations
> ho . . .

(Jack Wickert exits. A Spanish Friar in a monk robe enters and takes the roses away from the Flower Lady. He hands her a laptop computer and exits. She slowly opens the computer and begins to type. Behind her, a bright gobo slowly fades up and reads: HYPERLINK HTTP://WWW.MISSIONROSAS.COM.

Lights fade to black.)

The End

Anthems

CULTURE CLASH IN THE DISTRICT

WASHINGTON, D.C.

Introduction to
ANTHEMS: CULTURE CLASH IN THE DISTRICT

By Molly Smith

Culture Clash—three crazy masters of comedy—are quite seri-ous about the challenges of life in cross-cultural America. With a mission to increase cultural understanding, they illuminate and undermine all that pulls us apart. They expose our lives— full of passion, hot air and insecurity—set them on fire and then douse the whole flaming mass with a bucket of humor.

Ric, Herbert and Richard know first-hand the cross-cultural tensions of America. As young Latino/Chicano performers, they found their performance opportunities limited because as Richard says, "We never changed our names, wore blue con-tacts or watered down our material." I am delighted the Hollywood formula wasn't a fit for them, otherwise we might never have known the artistic comic genius that became Culture Clash. A creative collaboration, nineteen years old and going strong, Culture Clash enjoys an impressive partnership. Marriages and mergers rarely last that long.

I think of Culture Clash as a trio of Lenny Bruces storming the stage, holding an enormous mirror to our society. These the-ater artists are as comfortable talking on a sophisticated level about politics as they are at a rave (and able to switch quickly between the different worlds). Both outsiders and insiders of the culture, they get under the skin of a particular city by engaging communities with their interview process.

Their experiences in Washington, D.C. began during our 1999–2000 season, when Culture Clash came to Arena Stage with their Miami-based piece, *Radio Mambo*. While here, Arena commissioned the team to create for Washington, D.C. a site-specific exploration of the city similar to the one they created for Miami. Naming the project *Radio D.C.: Culture Clash in the District*, the team set about their task. Fanning out through the city, they interviewed any Washington resident within their range—from the powerful to the "everyman."

Two years into the process, the events of September 11th changed our world and, of course, the project. Because Washington was so affected by the attacks, the team knew right away that the piece would have to shift. Richard returned from Los Angeles to Washington immediately after the attacks, leaving Ric and Herbert with families who were afraid for them to travel during those tense days and weeks. Waiting for his flight in the Los Angeles airport, Richard happened to meet a grief counselor from Arlington, Texas, who was flying east to help families devastated by the events of 9/11. After a long, soulful conversation, the counselor encouraged Richard to search the city for an "anthem" for Washington, D.C. Because of that conversation, *Anthems: Culture Clash in the District* was born.

Exactly one year later, *Anthems* opened Arena's 2002–2003 season. Charles Randolph-Wright, who was an incredible match for the energy of Culture Clash, directed the production. Written by Richard Montoya and Culture Clash, the team used seven other actors as well as Ric and Richard (Herbert was with his project *Cantinflas!* in San Francisco) to create unforgettable characters who left their mark on Arena Stage and Washington, D.C.

The rehearsal process was unusual. Rehearsals in front of an audience were held, with the first one beginning just four days into the rehearsal process. The team read the play, and gauging audience reaction and comments, they molded the piece. Scenes were dropped, added and moved as the production found its final shape.

Anthems gives us an entirely unofficial and unauthorized tour of the city—shot through the lens of Culture Clash's wild comic imagination. We see some familiar faces and places, but mostly we encounter ordinary, everyday people we rarely see or hear onstage. It was important to show the real humanity of Washington, not just the president and senators. *Anthems* is about the complexity of feelings people have for their city, their country and each other during uncertain times. By the end, we laughed, we cried, we were provoked, and came closer to knowing the soul of Washington D.C.—the forgotten ground zero.

Living with culturally different neighbors is the American way of life. America is the great melting pot, as Mohammed, the Washington, D.C. cab driver in *Anthems* says: "My children are American—Muslim-American, Islamic-American—two worlds, two gods. They worship Allah and Nike." In our melting pot and over our divides, Culture Clash invites us to look at each other . . . and laugh our way to understanding.

Molly Smith *is the artistic director of Arena Stage.*

PRODUCTION HISTORY

Anthems: Culture Clash in the District was commissioned by Arena Stage (Molly D. Smith, Artistic Director; Stephen Richard, Executive Director), where it premiered in Washington, D.C., on September 4, 2002. The director was Charles Randolph-Wright; the set and lighting design were by Alexander V. Nichols, the costume design was by Anne Kennedy, the dresser diva was Kate Share, the sound design was by Timothy M. Thompson; the dramaturg was Michael Kinghorn and the stage manager was Pat A. Flora. The cast was Johanna Day, Bill Grimmette, Nikki Jean, Joseph Kamal, Richard Montoya, Jay Patterson, Psalmayene 24, Ric Salinas and Shona Tucker.

A NOTE ABOUT DESIGN

Alex Nichols created a very simple and elegant stage that was not really a set. Rows of lights at the foot of the stage mimicked the Metro lights of D.C.'s subway stations. The "mundane and the monumental" was our theme: it started in the streets, then it was in the script, then Alex built a set that at once looked like the monuments of D.C. but also served as platforms for the city's rushing and always busy population. Anne Kennedy designed hand-cut gray wool suits—this became our monochrome, our continuous, that invisible worker bee; again, simple elegant vocabulary that helped the play find itself. Tim Thompson's sound design captured the passing trains, the planes and the buzz of the Beltway. Miles Davis, Billie Holiday and the sounds of the National Zoo are not only essential but they put us squarely in the universe, the jungle that is D.C.

The National Zoo—2002

*In blackness we hear the 1970s soul jam "Rock Creek Park" by The
Blackbyrds.*

*Lights up to reveal Tian Tian, the beloved National Zoo panda bear,
chain-smoking. He wears a leather jacket, two-tone Stacy Adams patent
leather shoes and a simple panda mask. Music fades out.*

Tian Tian: What's up with the fuckin' cherry blossoms? What a
bunch of hype. You people need to decide, you want cherry
blossoms or panda? It's just a lot of pressure on Mei Xiang
and me, and let me tell you I got enough pressure on
already.

Everyday it's something: roll over, be cute, don't play
with your bamboo shoots, don't pet the snakehead fish,
take your West Nile Virus tablets, code-red air quality,
code-blue security, sign the petition for the incumbent
mayor. God I miss Marion Barry, used to get high with him
all the time . . . taxation without representation, I don't
even have a vote on the Hill for god sakes. I get no mer-
chandizing. And the one that really gets me—everyday they
say to me, "Make a baby!"

You know what? Bite me!

You make a baby with three hundred pimply face high
school kids watching you. It's an impossibility I tell ya.

(Tian Tian moves slowly onto all fours.)

I'm sorry people, I'm a wreck, it's a really mixed bag being the symbol for the Nation's Capitol. D.C. can be a real jungle and you people can be animals sometimes.

I feel useless really, I'm just a hack for the federal government when it comes right down to it.

I'm not even a GS-10 for crissakes . . . *(Yelling to offstage)* Everyone in Primate World's at least a GS-14! The reptiles are all GS-15s.

(Back to audience) They're not listening.

The zookeepers here are so anal and literal, high-strung, it's always *panda*monium around here. They're always coddling me with this endless feely touchy crap.

Please don't tell them I was smoking, they'll kick the crap out of me.

Get this, sometimes they play eleventh-century Chinese court music to calm me down. Let me tell you, nothing pisses me off more than eleventh-century Chinese court music. God. Put on some real music, a-holes!

(We hear a blast of Ozzy Osbourne. Tian Tian does air-guitar. He motions for the music to stop; it does. Abruptly, he slumps back down, leaning against his playpen, facing the audience.)

(Resigned) I don't even speak Chinese.

Look at me, I'm a black-and-white bear in a mostly black-and-white town.

Black patches, white patches, together, apart, slightly segregated, but in the same general area—there it is there.

Did you know I have the same heart doctor as Dick Cheney? True. He comes in from Bethesda once a month. I turn right, I turn left, I cough, he goes.

I'm somehow reminded of what my attorney James Fitzpatrick says. Fitz says, and I quote, "America's biggest tragedy is that Clarence Thomas is so young and healthy."

(A beat.)

Jeez, I didn't know it was Republican night.

I'm not sorry.

Let's change the subject, lighter topics I promise—a woman's right to choose, go!

Oh man, I need a mai tai, a mojito. Take me to Ben's Chili Bowl, get me a half-smoke.

Anybody wanna get animal tonight?

Ooh, I know. Look I know a terrific disco in Dupont Circle, we can all get on the VIP list and dance all night long with my gay brothers and sisters!

Was that too much information?

Wow, people, it's 2002.

Put it together! There are no panda babies because I'm a queer panda! I am a *home-ee*-sexual panda bear. Jeez, just let me be me. One day I swear I'm just gonna take my mask off. C'mon, D.C. is a very gay town, everybody here is gay . . . well, Ashcroft is not, but many others are. The jury is still out on Strom Thurmond, but some of his interns are. Condoleezza, come home baby girl!

This is terrific, I honor you for listening. My therapist will be so proud of me—I essentially just outted myself to you and I haven't even told my panda ol' lady about it. Let me say that she's a loyal Maoist so I don't think she'll be warming up to the idea of strap-ons anytime soon. Stay with me here people, we're about to lose the funding here.

The absolute strangest (and I suppose in some ways the most beautiful) thing about being me in a place like D.C., the Nation's Capitol, is that, well, I'm an immigrant, and you love me!

(We hear a commercial jetliner swoosh over Tian Tian. The lights change; we are now in the LAX Airport Terminal Bar.)

Los Angeles—September 16, 2001

We hear the continuing sound of a commercial airliner. Lights, airport sounds and Muzak.

Airport Announcer: Welcome to Los Angeles International Airport. Due to heightened security, please do not leave your bags unattended. All bags are subject to search . . .

(Airport sounds continue.
   We see a sky cap pushing an elderly black lady in a wheelchair across the entire length of the stage. Other travelers and airport security pass by.
   Ben Bull, a traveler, sits at an airport terminal bar. A bartender brings him a beer. He is joined by The Writer, who places his backpack next to his stool. He nervously sits, wanting to sip a beer, read his newspaper and, above all else, mind his own business. A beer is served to him. Ben Bull strikes up a conversation with The Writer.)

Ben Bull: I have to walk a family through the Pentagon in the morning. We've been allowed that. They will need that.
   An African-American family. A mother and father, and I guarantee you don't wanna be there.

(Extends his hand) Ben Bull, grief counselor from Arlington, Texas.

(They shake.)

The Writer: How are ya.

Ben Bull: Where ya headed, son?

The Writer: Dulles.

Ben Bull: Me, too. So, what takes you to Washington, D.C., so soon after . . .

The Writer *(Sheepishly)*: We're writing uh, a play about the Nation's Capitol.

Ben Bull: That's neat, wow. A play, huh? I've never written a play or a book or anything like that.

You said, "We're." "We're writing a play"?

The Writer: I usually write with two other fellas.

Ben Bull *(Looking around)*: Where are your partners? Can I buy them a beer?

The Writer: No. Their wives wouldn't let them travel so I'm flying solo on this one.

Ben Bull: Sounds like you got quite a task on your hands, young man. *(The Writer nods)* Well, I hope you find the heart, the life and the blood of that city, because I'll tell you what son, it's a wonderful place.

There is a "there" there.

(The Writer considers that line and then quickly reaches for a pencil in his inside lapel pocket to write it down, lest he forget it. He takes notes on his newspaper.)

And with the country so focused on New York City, D.C.'s gonna need something, so . . . *(Thoughtfully)* make it continuous.

(The Writer does not follow him. Ben Bull picks up on this.)

Your play. Make it continuous. Not chaos. It has to be continuous. The rage, the chaos—that's easy—we already know that stuff.

(The Writer writes.)

And after the dirge, after the requiems—and god I am going to dread all those requiems—make sure there is an anthem for us. Not just a call to war but an anthem, and I am not talking about a "National Anthem" necessarily or an anthem for the government or kings and queens, you understand. But an anthem for the regular guys. And make it continuous. Please. We're gonna need that.

The Writer: What do you mean "continuous"?

Ben Bull: Look, you are me and I am you. You have to be me, you must be me. I must be you. There have been a thousand deaths a thousand times this week . . . *(Points to the newspaper)* a thousand faces we will never know, yet we know who they are because they are us and we are them.

(The Writer furiously writes.)

Let me ask you a question.

The Writer: Sure. *(Reaches for his beer)*

Ben Bull: What would you say to a small child who runs up to every fireman she sees, thinking that fireman is her father?

(The Writer does not answer. He places his beer back on the counter.)

Yeah, you now have a glimpse into the complex world of this grief counselor from Arlington, Texas, and I don't care if you're as dumb as three rocks—it's going to hit you right here. *(Points to his heart)*

The Writer *(Carefully)*: I suppose in a place like Washington you just replace the fireman with a military person or postal worker?

Ben Bull: Exactly.

(A beat.)

When I first came back from Vietnam, the first time, two tours . . . *(Holds up two fingers)* when I heard a backfire from a passing car I would dive under a mailbox.

We do not wanna live that way, son.

You see this ribbon I have on my lapel? I fought and nearly died for this thing but I'll tell you a little secret, I made this ribbon from all the flags I found on the ground. People got bored with waving them and so they just tossed them on the floor I guess. *(Makes a waving gesture)* You dummies! You just don't throw flags on the ground, you take them home and burn them, you put them on the PaineWebber and grill if you have to and dispose of it in a proper fashion, but don't leave them on the—aagh!

I was at a ceremony last night, invited by the mayor of your fair Los Angeles, thank you very much, and they had the Black Children's Chorus that was just awful. They couldn't carry a tune in a water bucket but they were forcing it and just trying too hard, the poor little things.

And your mayor and his cronies have there, the Horse of the Fallen Rider, and well, I'll tell you what, the boots were not in the stirrups backwards, the reins were not cocked and the saddle was not fitted properly, so I left the ceremony disgusted. They were grandstanding and not paying attention to detail. This does not help.

Pay attention to detail friend.

The Writer: Yes, sir. *(Writes a quick note)*
Ben Bull: Where is your lapel ribbon, sir? *(Points to his lapel)*
The Writer: I don't wear flags.

(Ben Bull takes his ribbon off and gives it to The Writer.)

Ben Bull: I want you to have this . . .
The Writer: You don't have to do that, sir . . .
Ben Bull: You're gonna need it, son.
The Writer: That's OK . . . really, it's yours . . .
Ben Bull: Do I look like I will take no for an answer?
The Writer: Well . . .

(Ben Bull begins to pin the ribbon on The Writer's lapel, then stops for a moment.)

Ben Bull: I am assuming you are an American?

(The Writer nods affirmative and accepts the pin.)

The Writer: I am an American.

(Ben Bull pins the ribbon.)

Ben Bull: OK then.
The Writer: Look at that, that's . . . uh . . . neat. Thanks.
Ben Bull: De nada amigo. *(Backslaps The Writer)*
    So, when you finish writing this play, where will you be performing it, at the Kennedy Center?

(The Writer shakes his head no. Ben Bull considers this.)

The Writer *(Apologetically)*: No, no, we're not there yet.
Ben Bull: That's OK.

(Beat.)

Heck, I think the Kennedy Center looks like a big ol' Kleenex box. Ever noticed that?

(The Writer writes this down.)

Don't use that. God no, I know the director there, Mr. Kaiser. He's relatively new and we don't know if he has a sense of humor yet.

(The Writer erases the note.)

The Writer: Well, I definitely won't use that then.
Ben Bull: When you are done with this play, let me know and I'll send in my check or fly back and see it.

(Ben Bull gives The Writer a business card.)

The Writer: Sweet.
Ben Bull: I'll bring my wife.
The Writer: Excellent.
Ben Bull: Are you married?
The Writer: No, sir.
Ben Bull: Do you know what love is?

(The Writer lets the question hang there. He then gestures to Ben Bull for the answer.)

Love is when you're a big ol' gringo like me and you marry a nice Jewish girl, and get circumcised at age twenty-four!

(The Writer nearly spits out his beer.)

The Writer: Ouch.
Ben Bull: That, my friend, is love.

(A beat.)

The Writer: And love hurts.

(Ben Bull puts down a few bucks on the bar.)

Sorry buddy.
Ben Bull: Let me say this, on the record . . .

(The Writer gets back to writing.)

. . . there is nowhere on earth where by individual conceit you can just wipe out people, and that's all I have to say about that. *(Taps the table to punctuate his comment)*

The Writer: Got it.

Ben Bull: Whew, thank you sir, thank you for being my grief counselor just then.

The Writer: No worries.

Ben Bull: You got my words but I got your heart.

(Both men nod.)

I saw you go through airport security.

The Writer: Is that right?

Ben Bull: You were just ahead of me in the line there.

The Writer: No kidding?

Ben Bull: You got a weapon past the guards didn't you?

The Writer: My god don't even joke about that Ben . . .

Ben Bull: Yes you did.

The Writer: I did not, no sir.

Ben Bull: Yes you did!

(The Writer is confused.)

Your pen, your laptop, is a great weapon.

(A beat. The Writer downs what's left of his beer.)

You are not a playwright this week. No sir, this week you are a war correspondent.

The Writer: OK.

(The Writer quickly writes this down.)

Ben Bull: OK. You just learned a valuable lesson at a terrible price, so don't ever forget. *(The Writer nods)* Write this play, this orchestration or whatever it is, and in the last six bars or words or phrases give us our anthem. Give us that, I beg you, and if it sucks, make it better. Now, God bless.

The Writer: You, too.

Ben Bull: Be careful over there in the District.

(Ben Bull extends his hand for a shake.
They shake. Ben Bull yanks The Writer in close for a smother-ing bear hug. After a few slaps on the back, Ben Bull pulls away and begins to exit. The Writer adjusts his back. Ben Bull faces him.)

Hey, remember the anthem. Promise?

(The Writer nods. Ben Bull salutes The Writer militaristically, then disappears back into the nervous airport crowd. The Writer does a half-ass salute, while watching Ben Bull walk away. He reaches for his lapel pin and takes a deep breath. We hear more airplanes and airport sounds.
Lights fade.)

Dulles—September 17, 2001

Airport Announcer: Welcome to Dulles International Airport. Due to heightened security, please do not leave your bags unat-tended. All bags are subject to search . . .

Mohammed, a Muslim cab driver, enters downstage. There is Indian music and cab radio sounds. There are several long and uncomfort-able moments as The Writer tries to flag a cab down, which is pro-hibited at Dulles International Airport. Then:

Mohammed: Taxi, my friend?

(The Writer nods. Mohammed takes his bags. They move downstage.
Lights change abruptly. Music out. We hear the tires screech. In an instant, with a shift of lights, we are in Mohammed's cab.)

I will not be an apologist for my people. I do not speak offi-
cially for my people, OK my friend?

(The Writer fumbles for his tape recorder in his backpack.)

The Writer: OK . . .
Mohammed: I am American.

*(The Writer leans in from the backseat, pointing his tape recorder
at Mohammed.)*

For eighteen years I have been U.S. citizen. I speak only for
my heart. My family originally from Jordan. Some family
Palestinian from Ramallah, some Jordanian. Who are my
people I ask you? Who are your people, you look Middle
Eastern, right?
The Writer: Right.
Mohammed: My children are American—Muslim-American,
Islamic-American—two worlds, two gods. They worship
Allah and Nike.
　　My wife complain I not married to her, I am married to
taxi. Eighteen years in Washington D.C., I have seen it all
my friend. I have picked up senators, I have picked up
prostitutes, sometimes at the same time.
　　Every now and then I drive to Virginia but never Mary-
land. Never.
The Writer: What brought you to America . . . *(Looks at the visor
name tag)* Mohammed?
Mohammed: Yes, Mohammed. Freedom.
The Writer: Freedom?
Mohammed: I have respect for freedom you see. That's why we're
here. My children love it here. *(Reacts to a reckless driver who
has just cut him off; curses in Arabic)* Magnoosh! Son of a gun.
Look at that guy, he just cut me off like nothing . . . I always
look at the plates. See, Jersey plates. No respect, D.C.
means nothing to him. He go to Crystal City for sure.
The Writer: Crazy guy.
Mohammed: You think that's crazy?
The Writer: Yeah.

Mohammed: A man got into my cab day before yesterday. He ask me if I related to Osama bin Laden?

The Writer: Was it some sort of joke?

Mohammed: I assure you, my friend, it was no joke. He look at me very strange, I could feel his anger to me. I feel less than a human being. I not blame him. Never. Fear him yes, blame him no. Was he going to hurt me? I don't know. He ask again. At that moment, I was so scared, I pray . . . I finally say to him no, no sir, I not related to bin Laden.

For god sakes we are all Americans I say.

The Writer: What did he do?

Mohammed: He not look convinced.

People are angry. I don't know if things ever be normal again. What is normal? Maybe normal was not so good in the first place.

The Writer: These are confusing and dangerous times. What about your children? You mentioned kids.

Mohammed: My oldest son, also named Mohammed.

The Writer: Like you.

Mohammed: Right. Not a very good name to have in America this week. I take him to basketball game at MCI Center for his birthday. He go crazy for Michael Jordan, oh boy, and the Wizard cheerleaders, oh my god that kid! There is nothing in Koran about raising American teenager. This kid have friends all over the world—internet.

The Writer: How about you, you have friends, you get out much?

Mohammed: Oh sure, I have Salvadoran friends, Senegalese friends. I have one Israeli friend.

The Writer: Really?

Mohammed: Actually, just guy from the deli. Sometimes we argue, mostly we argue, other times we just look at each other unable to speak. Afraid tomorrow's news worse news than today, today's news worse than yesterday. Endless, hopeless . . . Yesterday he ask me . . .

(Yuri the Israeli enters, Mohammed stands. The lights shift abruptly. The men argue directly in front of the cab.)

Yuri: Does every Arab want every Jew dead?

Mohammed: I do not speak for all Arabs, but no, I say, no, god no.

(Yuri holds up a newspaper.)

Yuri: Jihad, everywhere jihad!

Mohammed: The only jihad I know is right here buddy. *(Points to his heart)* A jihad of my heart. There is a gosh-darn war in my own heart.

Yuri: Do you denounce terrorism, Mohammed?

Mohammed: Yes, Yuri, a thousand times yes!

Yuri: No more talking . . .

Mohammed *(Reaching out to Yuri)*: Yuri, Yuri, Yuri. Look, we all come from the same place my friend, we are cousins, Yuri . . . *(Boldly grabs Yuri's yarmulke and his own Muslim cap and holds them side by side. Facing Yuri)* and we are all going to the same place, we will all die one day my friend.

(Yuri grabs his yarmulke.)

Yuri: Shalom.

Mohammed: In-sha-allah.

(Yuri quickly exits. Mohammed puts his cap back on. He sits back in his cab. The lights shift.)

"Shalom," he say.

The Writer: Shalom.

Mohammed: Do you remember who say: "Give me liberty or give me death"?

The Writer: Yasir Arafat on CNN.

(After a beat.)

Mohammed: Ah no, my friend, America say this to the British. I know because this was question on my citizenship exam. Let me tell you something, my friend.

The Writer: Yes Mohammed.

Mohammed: Some people have come to mosque recently—American people, white people, even a rabbi from the temple.

The Writer *(Quietly)*: Wow.

Mohammed: Very brave—we grieve together, we pray together. This is beautiful thing. This is America to me.

The Writer: Yes.

(A light change.)

Mohammed: Here we are, my friend, Waterside Towers. Good luck.

The Writer: What's the damage there Mr. Mohammed?

Mohammed: OK, let me see, that was twenty-three zones you owe to me . . . only $582 my friend.

The Writer: What?

Mohammed: Ahh fucker guy!!!! *(Happy with his joke)*

(Mohammed exits.

A light change. First Metro train. The Writer slowly moves downstage. We hear the rush of the train, the Metro lights flicker. The Writer is joined by several Washingtonians. The train enters the station. There is a crack of thunder. Another light change. All exit.)

Georgetown Gala

Picture frames and a chandelier fly into place as breezy cocktail music sets the mood. The Host and Hostess enter dancing. The Host (African-American) and the Hostess (Waspy babe) take center stage.

Hostess: Ladies and gentlemen, donors and sponsors, patrons of the arts, thank you so very much for joining us this evening and welcome to our lovely home.

Host: As you all know, due to the tragic events of September, we've had to postpone our fundraiser for several months. However, Bunny and I felt strongly . . .

Hostess: . . . that if we didn't proceed with the gala, well then the terrorists win.

(Applause from backstage.)

And without your generous support, we would have never met our fundraising goals for the National Zoo's panda fertility program!

Host: Enough business, I wanna see everybody on the dance floor, enjoying the Hispanic music . . .

Host and Hostess: . . . let's do the D.C. Tango!

(Tango music. Party guests, along with party servers dressed in Civil War-era Union jackets and hats, enter. Everybody dances the tango. The Host takes center stage.)

Host: Listen folks, we are very honored this evening to be joined by the Tajikistani Ambassador to the United States. *(Applause)* Your Excellency?

(The Ambassador enters with a woman in a full burqa.)

Ambassador: Thank you, Thomas and Bunny. And thank you for having us in your lovely home. And thank you, Bunny, we are using the same architect for our embassy.

(Bunny bows humbly to the Ambassador.)

Let me assure all Americans that my country will do everything in her power to find and liquidate Mr. Osama bin Laden. We will find him . . . *(Looks at his companion, who holds up her index finger)* in one week!

(Tango music. Photo flashes. The Host moves toward a Senator.)

Senator: Hey, Tommy, I want that son of a bitch ambassador frisked from turban to toe.

Host: Very well, Senator.

(Tango music continues. The Hostess and Diva Tamer move in close for some chit-chat.)

Hostess: Darling, did you get your botox shots?

Diva Tamer *(With a stiff face)*: Yes, and I feel wonderful.

Hostess: You look so natural.

(Tango music continues. The Writer swoops in on Diva Tamer. They dance across the stage and converse.)

Diva Tamer: I understand you are writing a play about the District of Columbia?
The Writer: That's correct, ma'am.
Diva Tamer: Is your play somewhere we can see it?
The Writer *(Proudly)*: It's at Arena Stage.
Diva Tamer: I'm so sorry. I don't do southwest D.C.

(The Writer moves near the Senator.)

The Writer: Senator, may I ask you a question?
Senator: Off the record?
The Writer: Absolutely.
Senator: Shoot.
The Writer: When will the U.S. bomb Baghdad?
Senator: In November, about a week before the mid-term elections.

(Diva Tamer catches the arm of The Writer.)

Diva Tamer: I trust you'll capture things accurately, young man? Here in Washington, we work on the honor system

*(The Writer listens to the cocktail conversations all around him and takes notes.
    Diva Tamer to Hostess:)*

Did you know so and so is fucking senator so and so?
Hostess: Those busy Democrats.

(A Server in Civil War garb to the Senator:)

Server: Senator, did President Bush steel the election?
Senator: Yeah. Jesus Christ.

(Hostess squeezes in next to The Writer.)

Hostess: I've been wanting to ask you, is your play about 9/11?

(The Writer looks to the Host and the Senator, who shoot him a look. The tango music stops. The party comes to an uncomfortable standstill.)

The Writer: I don't think we can avoid the issue.
Hostess: My brother was in Tower Two . . .
The Writer: I'm very sorry . . .
Hostess: Oh no. He got out, thank God.

Host *(Changing the subject)*: Ladies and gentlemen, since Latin music is our theme tonight, our dear amigo and kitchen captain from El Salvador will demonstrate the finer points of salsa dancing! —José!

(There is applause and encouragement for José.)

José *(Humbly)*: No, no. Thank you sir, I'm too busy . . . OK.

(José hands his serving tray to The Writer, who temporarily becomes a server.)

OK, OK. Tonight I will show you the different ways people in Washington, D.C., dance salsa. For example, in Columbia Heights when Salvadoreños dance salsa they move their big nalgas. They shake their booties.

Puerto Ricans know how to dance salsa. They invented it—any Cubans here? But when they dance it looks like they are thinking, Did I leave the iron on?

Now the black people, when they dance salsa, the music might be jamming. But they go like this: *(Does slow-jam movements)*

Haaay! Now when white people dance salsa—no, no, we shouldn't discourage them! I know they have it in them, they know how to dance that Riverdance stuff . . . *(Does a Riverdance jig)* But when they dance, it looks like this: *(Does a hippie-type dance with his right hand flailing high above his head. Looking at his hand)* What the fuck is this? They think they're still in Woodstock.

(The gala comes to a stop.)

Thank you very much—I find another job now. *(Exits)*
Host: Musica!!

*(We hear a blast of salsa music. The party people exit, the woman
in the burqa whips off her garb to reveal a beautiful red dress. She
salsas wildly. The Ambassador, scandalized, chases her out.*
*We now hear the marching music of John Philip Sousa as the
lights change.)*

The Madhatter of Capitol Hill

*We see Lincoln's image on the new five dollar bill as the music plays.
The Writer sits at a table, headbanging along.*
*Bill Fleishell, an eighty-three-year-old, eighth-generation
Washingtonian, who has lived in and around Capitol Hill since
his birth in the early twenties, enters. He carries a huge cardboard
logo of the Republican Party. Music out.*

The Writer: What ya got there, Bill?
Bill Fleishell: I spent thirty years drawing elephants for the
Republican National Committee, I did. Some people like it,
some people don't.

A friend of mine said, "Hey, the Republican Party is
looking for an art director." I said I'm interested. Art director for the Republican Party? I didn't know there was such
a job. Sounds like an oxymoron.

(The Writer agrees. Bill places the large logo on the table.)

I want you to take this back with you.
The Writer: I will cherish this.
Bill Fleishell: Let me tell you, I met everybody. We handled Barry
Goldwater's campaign, Nixon, Eisenhower, Bob Dole.
Here's a picture of a young Bob Dole. Looks like Walter
Mondale there, god forbid. Jesse Helmes . . .
The Writer: With Noriega.

Bill Fleishell: Kissinger . . .

The Writer: With Pinochet.

Bill Fleishell: There's Rumsfeld.

The Writer: With the Sha of Iran.

Bill Fleishell: I don't have any pictures of Colin Powell. I really like him. Lots of wisdom, a real warrior.

(Looking at the photos as if they are baseball trading cards) A lot of those people are gone now. That's why I keep their pictures on the wall there, next to my peppers from the garden.

(Bill leaves momentarily and reenters with a huge bushel of red peppers.)

Here, take some peppers home, I got more than I need.

The Writer: Thank you, I'll put them right on the elephant here.

Bill Fleishell: Did you go to the Eastern Market yet?

The Writer: No I haven't.

Bill Fleishell: You gotta go!

The Writer: I'll make a note of it.

Bill Fleishell: Lots of history all around, kid. I don't know what else to tell you.

My son's an engraver at the Bureau of Engraving. He engraved the new five dollar bill. Have you got a five dollar bill?

(The Writer produces a five dollar bill. Bill holds the bill up to the light for inspection.)

Isn't that snappy? Look at that. Big-headed Lincoln. My boy did that.

(The Writer reaches for his money, but Bill puts the five in his pocket.)

My son lives in the alley behind John Philip Sousa. Lots of history. Just a few steps away really.

The Writer: Now Sousa wrote some anthems.

Bill Fleishell: He's the "King of the Anthems." Now my great-grandfather lived at 17, 3rd Street Southeast, where the

Foldger Theater is. And my great-uncle died in the Civil War Naval Hospital down the street. Well, I don't know what else to tell you . . . eight generations in Capitol Hill, Fleishell's the name. Just thought you might want to know that.

Did you go to the Eastern Market?

The Writer: Not yet.

Bill Fleishell: You gotta go!

The Writer: I'll make a note of it.

Bill Fleishell: For what it's worth, I have this relationship to Christine Todd Whitman. When I first met her she was just a rich kid from northern New Jersey. Anyway, one of her relatives was an admiral by the name of Sleigh: S-L-E-I-G-H. He was instrumental in signing a peace treaty between Spain and America during the Spanish-American war. That peace treaty was signed right here on this wooden table . . .

The Writer: Whoa . . .

Bill Fleishell: . . . priceless. Come down here and look for yourself.

(Bill climbs under the table and shows The Writer the table signature.)

C'mon down here, son. See that, signed by a Spaniard. You're Spanish, right kid?

The Writer: Oh sure . . .

Bill Fleishell: What's that say right there?

The Writer: Manufactured by IKEA employees.

Bill Fleishell: Watch your head.

(The Writer bangs his head hard on the underside of the table.)

Look out!

(The Writer hits his head again.)

Look out! We better sit down before somebody kills themselves.

(They sit back down. A phone rings.)

The Writer: Your phone is ringing.

Bill Fleishell: Ha?

The Writer: Your phone is ringing, sir.

Bill Fleishell: Ha?

The Writer: Your phone or my head is ringing incessantly.

Bill Fleishell: Oh, I'm not gonna get it. It's probably Condoleezza again.

I just don't know what else to tell you.

(Bill reaches for a small wooden box and places it on the table.)

Here's some more things I wanted to show you . . . *(Pulls out a feathered pen)* This is a pen that was used to sign the Declaration of Independence. *(Pulls out an old iron key)* Here's the key Ben Franklin used to discover electricity . . . *(Hands the key to The Writer; it shocks the hell out of him)* Still got some juice in her. *(Pulls out an old pistol)* This is a pistol from the Civil War, just got it back from Ken Burns.

The Writer: It's a beauty.

Bill Fleishell: You'll get a kick out of this. *(Pulls out a theater program)* This is a program from a play called *Our American Cousin*. That's the play President Lincoln was watching the night he was assassinated by a subscriber—I mean an actor—John Wilkes Booth, the actor. I thought you might want to know that.

I don't know what else to tell you.

Did you go to the Eastern Market yet?

The Writer: I was there about an hour ago, Bill.

Bill Fleishell: Good. Come on into the study and I'll show you something.

The Writer: What'cha got in the study, Bill?

Bill Fleishell: It's the first dress ever worn by J. Edgar Hoover.

(Bill exits.

A light change. On another part of the stage, we see three actresses performing the Victorian-era play Our American Cousin. *The ladies wear brightly colored bonnets and hoop skirts.*

The Writer sits just behind a silhouetted President Lincoln in top hat and coat, who is watching the play.)

Georgina: Miss Florence, will you be kind enough to tell Dundreary about that American relative of yours.

Florence: My American cousin? Certainly. Well, he's about seventeen-feet high.

Dundreary: Good gracious, seventeen-feet high?

Florence: Yes, that's the average height in America. And they have long black hair that reaches down to their heels, and they have dark copper-colored skin. And they fight with tomahawks and scalping knives.

(Dundreary faints. President Lincoln and The Writer laugh.)

Quick, somebody throw a pail of water on her.

Georgina: No not that, she's pale enough already!

(President Lincoln and The Writer laugh.)

Florence: Don't be afraid Dundreary. I'll be by your side.

(President Lincoln and The Writer laugh. The Writer moves to stand just behind the president.)

I will protect you.

(President Lincoln applauds and laughs.)

(The Writer lifts the Civil War pistol to the back of Lincoln's head. It fires.
Loud thunder crack.)

The Writer: Oh my god, Mr. President . . .

(Lights change. The Writer, standing there with the pistol and the program, has become Booth the assassin. Lights out on Lincoln and the actresses. The Writer looks at the pistol for a moment and then runs off.)

American Nightmare

Droning music. Lights up slowly as an Anglo-American man enters pointing a double-barreled shotgun at the audience. He makes his way center stage in a pinspot special. He speaks directly to the audience:

American *(In a low, dramatic tone)*: They're out there, I feel 'em. Sand-niggers, evil camel jockeys, little ragheads planning and scheming their next attack on America. I feel 'em I tell ya. They're probably just off the interstate in some flea-bag motor lodge in Maryland. They're out there, I know it.

I'm gonna find 'em and shoot every last one of 'em evil bastards. Tom Ridge is gonna pin a badge on me, give me a three-foot trophy and that ain't no bragg-aday-cheeyo neither, I tell ya.

(The American is joined by an African-American, wearing an aluminum hat and holding a fifth of Jack Daniel's.)

African-American *(Truly afraid)*: C'mon now, you're freaking me out, Leeland. My wife is gonna call the sheriff's and I can't say that I blame her. Now come on neighbor, give me the freakin' firearm.

(The African-American reaches for the American's shotgun. There is slight resistance.)

American: Vern, you gotta trust me on this one—they're out there man.

(Lights come up on another area of the stage. Three Arabic-American men sit around a hookah.)

African-American: Ain't nobody out there. Now for the last time, give me the gosh-darn rifle.
American: They're out there, sure as hell. And they're better organized than the goddamned FBI.
African-American: Give me the gun, Lee.

(The American gives the African-American the shotgun without struggle.)

Jesus Christ. Let's go in.
American: Hold on.

(The American raises his hand chest high, as if he has heard something in the hedges. They freeze in fear and excitement.
Lights shift to the three Arabic-American men.)

Yusef: OK, guys, good meeting. I have to go, enshallah, bye-bye.
Mohammed: Be careful out there, guy.
Yusef: I be fine. You worry too much.
Mohammed: No really, I mean it, be very careful, Yusef. They are out there.
Yusef: There is nobody there. You worry too much, Mohammed.
Mohammed: No really, I can feel them, they hate us. The government will hunt us all down and arrest us.
Kamal: We are American citizens. That could never happen here.
Mohammed: No? Look at this . . . *(Holds up the* Washington Post, *reads headline)* "Washington Post, U.S. authorities investigating five hundred Muslim and Arab stores."

(Yusef grabs the newspaper and glances over it.)

Yusef: Mohammed, I send money home every year, this is routine.
Mohammed: My brother owns store, he has done nothing wrong!
(Getting excited)
Yusef: Take it easy, guy.
Mohammed: No! They look at us and see only bin Laden. *(Facing the audience)* They are out there, planning and plotting to hurt us.
Yusef: You are imagining things in your mind, fucker-guy.
Mohammed: I mean it, they have so much hate for us all. *(Getting more excited)* They're out there, I can feel it.
American: They're out there, I can feel it.
Kamal: You are paranoid, man.
African-American: Paranoid.
Yusef: Crazy guy.

American: Maybe it's a good thing this whole mess happened, Vern.

Mohammed: Bush, Sharon—watch, Iraq is next.

American: We needed a wake-up call, neighbor. We got fat in the belly. *(Like Mohammed, he faces the audience)*

Mohammed: Bombs for oil.

American: Let's nuke 'em.

Mohammed *(Simultaneously)*: They're out there. I can feel 'em.

American *(Simultaneously)*: They're out there. I can feel 'em.

(We hear the swoosh of the Metro. Blackout.)

Cisero Jones—Go-go History

Cisero addresses the audience:

Cisero Jones: See what happened was, is that years ago, before I turned my life around, I was locked-up right, up Lorton back in the early '70s, and we was all down in the cafeteria and these motherfuckers tried to feed us moldy bread, man—for the third day in a row. And I said—young revolutionary that I was—forget this man, we gon' protest. So I started bangin' on the table right, and then Rico and Killer, they started bangin', too.

And then the white boys, they table start bangin' too. And soon everybody in the cafetria was bangin' on the tables, sayin': "Fresh bread, fresh bread, fresh bread."

And in the midst of my bangin', somethin' overcame me—it was a possession that caused a polyrhythmic shift in my body and it came out like . . . and everybody else picked up on it, and Killer go, "Rico go . . . white boys, too . . ."

It was spiritual, man, real deep. So the next day, Saturday, was our visiting day, so Chuck, Chuck Brown, came out to visit me cuz we was real tight, grew up together, so I knew Chuck had a band and he would appreciate the experience. So I did the beat for him like . . . and at the time, I used to stutter right, since then I've gon' to speech therapy and it all corrected . . .

(The Writer enters.)

. . . so I told him, "Go, go, go, go, g, g, go, go, go out there and tell your bandmates about this man." Next thing I know, Chuck Brown discovered a new musical genre called go-go. And that's how go-go music was born in D.C.!

The Writer: Wow.

Cisero Jones: Maybe go-go's your anthem?

The Writer: Maybe so.

Cisero Jones: How do I get outta here man?

The Writer: Just follow me, Mr. Jones.

Cisero Jones: Yeah, yeah, thanks, thanks.

(Cisero Jones exits in the opposite direction of The Writer.
    The Writer is now at the Vietnam War Memorial with an African-American Vietnam Vet. The Vet wears a black cowboy hat, patches on his vest and a cardboard sign around his neck that reads: TOURS FOR FOOD. The Writer wheels the Vet slowly across the stage. We hear the song "The Night They Drove Old Dixie Down."
    Ben Bull enters. He addresses the audience:)

Ben Bull: Remember to go to the Vietnam Memorial wall. You'll likely find an old soldier there who's trying to remember those names on that wall forever, and forever keeps getting closer for him.

(Ben Bull walks off. The Vet, helped by The Writer, tries to rise out of his chair to touch the wall. The Vet collapses back into his chair, crying inconsolably. The Writer, not knowing what to do, slowly wheels the Vet offstage. We hear more of "The Night They Drove Old Dixie Down.")
    Sound of a paper shredder. Then:)

Give us that anthem, son. Make it continuous.

(The Writer appears with a large, clear plastic bag of shredded papers.)

The Writer *(Looking up)*: Thanks for the abstraction Ben Bull . . .

    (To the audience) OK folks, I've been all over the District on this journey of ours. I have been to the Cloak Room, the Senate Library, the Federal Reserve and the World Bank, and I'm thinking that our anthem may lay somewhere in this pile of shredded documents.

(Picks up shreds of paper and "reads" them:)

Nothing but funny numbers. *(Another shred)* Do not destroy, Department of Finance . . . *(Another)* This little pink one is about Martha Stewart, it's a very greedy thing . . . Well . . . now this is weird, here's an interview I conducted just yesterday with a Panamanian fella.

(A Panamanian Man steps from the shadows. He speaks directly to the audience. His words are simultaneously translated by The Writer.)

Panamanian: I am from Panamá . . .

The Writer *(Translating)*: What this university professor and Embassy Row consultant is saying, his words now . . . "When he saw those planes fly into the buildings in New York City and Washington D.C., it brought great joy to his heart, a pleasure he could hardly contain himself."

Panamanian: . . . your president, President Bush, he killed thousands of people here in Panamá . . .

The Writer *(Translating)*: He says Panama City was destroyed in one night looking for one man we put in power in the first place, thousands of innocent Panamanians died he says. Finally he says the unsayable . . .

Panamanian: Muerte a los Americanos.

The Writer *(Translating)*: Death to the Americans.

(The Panamanian exits.)

Wow, we could never put that onstage.

(Hard Hat Guy enters.)

Hard Hat Guy: I'd like to knock that guy's block off, but I won't. He has a right to say shit like that in this country. I'd never celebrate anybody getting murdered. You shoulda seen the ocean of hard hats, guys that just showed up to the Pentagon—cutters, burners, fitters, welders, certified guys, guys from the local, black guys from Kentucky, white guys from Pennsylvania, contractors and laborers of every stripe. I was so proud . . . *(Stops to contain himself)* People died, people died . . . Remember that the next time some jerk-off runs his mouth.

The Writer: Here's a mother . . .

(A West African Woman enters holding an infant.)

West African Woman:
> Come to America,
> Work hard,
> Pay taxes,
> September happen
> Lose job,
> Tourists disappear,
> No hotel work,
> Seventy thousand hotel workers
> With no jobs,
> No airport work,
> No janitor work,
> No little jobs
> To feed little mouths.

(She exits.)

The Writer: Some people need jobs more than they need anthems, Ben.

> I'm just picking
> Up little bits here,
> Like a Forensic poet
> But it's not adding up
> To anything close to
> An anthem.

(The Writer pulls out a large, collard green leaf.)

There's that interview I wrote on a collard green . . . It's a clue . . . *(Holds the collard green up to the sky like an offering)* See, "Purple Mountain Majesties" on this side and the Jim Crow laws on the back. I will save this so I never forget. *(Puts the large collard green leaf in his pocket)* This is akin to being a deejay or an MC, if you will. See, I'm sampling, mixing, remixing our urban realities. Right here yo, shit I am hip-hop yo!

Let me kick it to you like this yo!
Searching for the anthem, night and day . . .
Went to the zoo and the panda was . . .

(Audience finishes line:)

Audience: Gay!

The Writer *(Incredulously)*: It's a goddamned Eminem concert in here. You people are homophobic.

(The Writer picks up his plastic bag filled with paper shreds and exits. Jaylee Mead, an elderly, sophisticated Washingtonian with short cropped hair, speaks directly to the audience:)

Jaylee Mead: You'll find that people in this town are very different. On the surface you'll find points of commonality to be sure, but below the surface you'll find deviations—I don't want to say deviants, but . . .

I've lived in this area all of eight years. D.C. Proper. But I lived in Maryland for over thirty years. Greenbelt, which is a whole other world. Greenbelt was built in the '30s. Eleanor Roosevelt was instrumental in it. It was a blue-collar community. Some might say it was socialistic in nature. There were only two others in the entire country (these planned and designed, very Anglo communities), one was in Pennsylvania. And the other is the Pentagon (that was a joke.)

I was a scientist out at NASA Goddard Space Flight Center, so I was a part of the community of mostly scientists. I was also at the State Department for six years.

I have a spotty past.

Washington is just so, oh, there is just so much here and most of it is free that you can go to—the theater is not free but all the museums are. I hope you take time to see those things. Most people in D.C. are too busy with their lives and pending indictments to go.

The District is the second most desirable place to live right after Salt Lake City, Utah. Good heavens, I don't know who would want to live in Utah.

(The Writer enters with a video camera and records Jaylee.)

I would strongly suggest that you go and visit Anacostia.

The Writer: Really?

Jaylee Mead: Oh yes. Why do you have that look on your face?

The Writer: Just things I've heard.

Jaylee Mead: Anacostia is a wonderful place. The Anacostia Museum is there and my good friend is the director, and I am sure he would be happy to show you around. There are a great many good things coming to Anacostia, young man.

The Writer: Yes, ma'am.

Jaylee Mead: It's not true and it's unfair to say that Anacostia is unsafe. Some people won't go there after ten P.M. Listen, I wouldn't go to the White House after ten P.M.

Take the Greenline there.

The Writer: The Greenline.

Jaylee Mead: My husband says I'm Pollyanna but I love this town. I feel I can almost wrap my arms around it.

We must always look for the good because you are more apt to find it. I am never down because I am afraid I will never get up!

Last year I was in Coooba . . .

The Writer *(Reacting to Jaylee's proper Spanish)*: Very good.

Jaylee Mead: With the Washington Ballet and recently was involved in a play reading myself. It was a fundraiser for one of the theaters here in the District, and I read a monologue from *Sweet Potato Queens*. The role calls for a southern accent but I was directed just to read it straight. *(The Writer asks for more)* Well, it was a piece about how to turn a man on. It was embarrassing for some, because it was a bit off-color. It's about a group of women from Mississippi (I think it is), and the women are talking about what is the best thing you can promise a man. Six women all sitting around a man. And of course I read my part with big pauses, leading up to it, very dramatic and all. And I say, "What we are all going to do is give you a . . . blow job!" Oh, it was great fun. Very Clintonian actually. I just love interacting with people.

The Writer: Do you consider yourself a patriot, Jaylee?

Jaylee Mead: Am I a patriot? Are you trying to trip me up, young man?

The Writer: No ma'am.

Jaylee Mead: Well, at the risk of sounding Clintonian what is your definition of a patriot?

The Writer: You tell me.

Jaylee Mead: It's certainly an interesting question.

We were at the White House once during the Bush presidency, the senior Bush, not the rocket scientist Dubya. And Mr. and Mrs. Bush are there and we're posing for a picture, and Mr. Bush is really tall, much taller than yours truly. Well, Mr. Bush reaches over and grabs my hand and says, "If they're going to take our picture we may as well be holding hands." And he grabs my hand like so. *(Demonstrates)* And we are holding hands and it was such a shock, to have him, you know, grab my hand like that. I just had this Cheshire grin on my face. Kinda gave me the willies. I took umbrage.

A Cheshire grin indeed.

(We hear a honk.)

Well, there's my Pakistani cab driver. Today we are discussing Muslim-Hindu politics.

(Jaylee begins to exit, stops to face The Writer.)

Did you know that Islam means peace?

Mecca

Arabic music and the Muslim call to prayer. We see a large crescent moon. A male figure slowly becomes clear to us. Other Muslim men are at prayer. A large star is added to the moon. It is the Islamic religious symbol.

The Man is Mohammed, the cab driver from earlier. He slowly comes nearer to us, holding a piece of paper over his chest. He lays down a Washington Post *newspaper as a prayer rug, takes off his sneakers and bends to his knees. He prays in the direction of Mecca. We are in a mosque.*

He unfolds the paper. It is a child's crayon drawing of the American flag. It reads GOD BLESS AMERICA. *He holds this up to his chest for all to see, then folds it and puts it in his pocket.*

Arabic writing is projected on the floor with the use of lighting gobos.

An Anglo couple wearing matching Washington Redskins jackets joins Mohammed. Mohammed rises to his feet. There is a greeting. The couple, Mr. and Mrs. Wilson from Friendship Heights, are visiting Mohammed at his mosque.

Mrs. Wilson: Mohammed . . .

(Mohammed gives the Wilsons the child's drawing.)

Mohammed: My daughter make for you, Mrs. Wilson.
Mrs. Wilson *(Accepting the drawing)*: Thank you.

(Mr. Wilson surprises Mohammed with a Washington Redskins jacket. Smiles all around.)

Mohammed: Oh my, thank you so much, my friends. Oh my, I really love the Redskins, my goodness this is too much, I could never . . . *(Puts on the jacket. Smiles all around)*
Mr. Wilson: Nonsense, it's already got your name on it. See?

(Mr. Wilson points out Mohammed's name on the jacket.)

Mohammed: I spell my name with "O" not "U," but that's OK.
Mrs. Wilson: I told him that, Mohammed. We argued at Tyson's Corner for two hours.
Mr. Wilson: Oh, it don't matter.
Mrs. Wilson: Well, how would you like it if somebody misspelled your name?
Mr. Wilson: Pipe down honey, we're in a church.
Mrs. Wilson: We're in a mosque, honey.
Mr. Wilson: Really? I thought it was a Dairy Queen.
Mrs. Wilson: Don't get cute.

Mr. Wilson: Does your wife talk back to you, Mohammed?

Mohammed: Oh yes.

Mrs. Wilson: Good for her.

Mohammed: I have to keep this jacket away from my son.

Mr. Wilson: You tell that little suicide bomber to keep his mitts off this jacket.

Mrs. Wilson: Honey.

(Mohammed subdues many emotions here; Mrs. Wilson, with a smile, is trying her best.)

Mr. Wilson: Just a joke.

Mohammed: I hope the Redskins have better season this year.

Mrs. Wilson: From your lips to God's ears.

Mr. Wilson: Allah's ears.

Mrs. Wilson: Oh Christ.

Mr. Wilson: Let's pray for the Deadskins.

Mohammed: Very well. We pray for the Redskins. Go for it.

(Mohammed goes to his knees to pray. This literal interpretation catches the Wilsons off-guard, but Mrs. Wilson gladly complies, pulling her husband, ol' big mouth, down with her. We hear the Arabic music reprieve as they all pray in the direction of Mecca.
A light change.)

Jesus Time!

Gospel music. A Christian cross slowly replaces the Islamic symbol of the star.
A dapper Preacher Man enters with The Writer.)

Preacher Man: Churches are like McDonald's or Wendy's. I mean, if you are off in a foreign country and you don't know anybody or know anything and you look up and see McDonald's, you might be tempted to go in there even though you might not like that hamburger.

Connections.

Overall it's an effort to reevaluate and to refine something about life. Many people come back to the churches in Washington, D.C., to find themselves. The flock gets scattered, the flock returns.

(The Preacher Man and The Writer are joined by an offstage congregation, the "Amen Corner," who responds to the Preacher Man.)

If you go back and look at the history of black people in the South and you were living on a plantation, the only escape was in the church. This was the appeal of the Baptist: independence, freedom, and they could seek out their own lives.

I don't know what your experience has been in growing up. But the general kind of experience in growing up in the South for white people was that: you're white, life is good, you're better than other folk. And God has blessed you and has smiled on you and Jesus is white and so forth.

Now, if you got an intelligent child who grows up in the South and goes off to college someplace, and he begins to study some geography or what not . . . he or she will soon realize that Jesus was over there in the Middle and Far East and so forth. And then you begin to figure if Jesus was blue-eyed, blond and so forth, how in the world did he get there? It is impossible! How can they get this in their mind, without any sense of geography to conclude that Jesus was a white man. It's an impossibility!

As a pastor I don't care what he was. Growing up in the church back in Alabama, for anybody to have done anything to desecrate the image of Christ would have been awful. To suggest, that Jesus was black or something would have been awful.

But, when you begin to examine all the Eurocentric theology, the essence of divinity—was Jesus as he appeared or how he was presented or how he evolved through the years? Going back to the old carvings and drawings, one has to ask oneself how on earth did Jesus go from looking like Osama bin Laden to Pat Boone?

(Thunder. The Preacher Man looks warily up toward the sky.)

Easy now . . .

(The Writer slowly walks closer to the Preacher Man, who proceeds cautiously.)

. . . the Jesus who was presented to me was a lie.

(More rolling thunder.
The Preacher Man and The Writer exit.)

In Heaven

An American Airlines Pilot stands in a pinspot and faces the audience. We hear only the sound of the Metro train. The Pilot's voice is amplified with a small mike so he can whisper.

Pilot: I'm in heaven. I'm in heaven with Neanderthals, samurai and wives. And if I remember living, it's like having a small itch, or humming something while you remember something else or forget something else. It doesn't matter because in heaven, everyone is equal.

When I died, the sound of the engine exploding was sustained throughout time. Who was I while I was alive? I don't remember.

I said to myself, I'm an American, and in that same precious instant I said, What is an American? I don't remember.

The population of heaven is young, brown, and does not speak much English. I have found very few "Americans" here.

There are no flags in heaven.

Everyone here seems to be black, Latin, Arab and Chinese. So I guess heaven is like earth. And D.C. was becoming more like heaven every day. But I didn't see it that way while I was alive.

Everything I remember, everything I forget. The socks under the bed, the crickets at night, the way the sun shined on my grandfather's balding head, creating a rainbow.

And if I could cry, I would cry ten lifetimes for the smoothness of the stones that I used to skip and more for the ones I kept in my pocket.

I guess I'm still unraveling all of these things that I will remember, and all those things that are burning, burning into forget.

(We hear the swoosh of the Metro. The Pilot exits. Lights out.

We hear the voice of Marian Anderson singing "God Bless America" at the Lincoln Memorial, mixed with snippets of historical audio:

Senator Joe McCarthy
MLK on the Mall
FDR's Day of Infamy
The death of JFK
Oklahoma City Bombing
Air strikes on Iraq
Persian Gulf Conflict.
This ends with a swoosh of the Metro train.)

100% Pure

Lights up on Ngozay Robertson talking to The Writer.

Ngozay: There was this white man named Claude Brown, he died about ten years ago. Our name is Brown, his name is Brown. Our families worked on the Brown Plantations in the South. We were relatives. At our fiftieth family reunion Claude Brown shows up. The reunion was where I spent all my summers: Ware Neck, Virginia. It's a little hick town in the tidewater basin that time forgot.

So we're having this big reunion and Claude Brown is sitting out in his car. So Gramma says:

(Granny enters.)

Granny: Claude Brown, you know this is silly, why don't you just come into the family reunion!

(Lights up on Claude Brown.)

Claude *(Very slow and thoughtful):* I don't know Miss Brown, reckon I'll just sit here in my automobile.
Granny: Suit yourself, Claude Brown. I'll send out a hot plate for ya.
Claude: Thank you kindly, Grandma Brown.
Granny: You're sure welcome, Claude Brown. Ya old fool.

(Granny exits.)

Ngozay *(Repeating Granny):* "Ya old fool."

Nobody in my family wants to admit that this white man is our relative. See, I have this social theory.
The Writer: OK.
Ngozay: People and their families prefer to see themselves as pure, 100% pure. Hello? What is that?

We have whites in our family, we have Indians in our family—I've seen pictures of Uncle Joe standing in front of his damn tepee.

It all came to a head for me a few weeks ago.

The Writer: What happened?

Ngozay: I took my mother to Lynchburg. Lynchburg, Virginia. You know, a day with Mom, outdoors, sunshine and no arguing about my hair.

(Ngozay's Mother enters.)

Ngozay's Mother: When are you gonna give the world a break, child?

Ngozay: I didn't know I was assaulting the rest of the world by keeping my hair like this.

Ngozay's Mother: Why you wearing that thing on your head?

Ngozay: Don't start, Mom.

Ngozay's Mother: Your auntie was one of the first women in D.C. with the Jerry Curl you know.

Ngozay *(Explaining to audience)*: A Jerry Curl Pioneer Woman.

Ngozay's Mother: Hush now, here comes the pretty lady, child.

(Lights shift. Enter a woman with a bright bonnet and period dress.)

Bonnet Lady: Welcome to the Lynchburg Historical Society walking tour. We are standing in the old town dairy barn, which has been restored to its eighteenth-century origins.

Ngozay's Mother *(To Ngozay)*: How lovely, child.

Ngozay: Uh-hum.

Bonnet Lady: This is an actual butter churner used by the dairy farmers . . .

Ngozay *(Interrupting)*: Where are the slaves?

Bonnet Lady: Pardon me?

Ngozay: The slaves?

Ngozay's Mother: Hush, child.

Bonnet Lady: The women folk of the farm would gather with the children . . .

Ngozay: Where are the slaves?

Ngozay's Mother: Hush, child.

Bonnet Lady: Perhaps you would like to churn the butter?

Ngozay: What?

Ngozay's Mother: Churn the butter, child.

Ngozay *(To Mother)*: I asked her a question. Where are the slaves, ma'am?

Bonnet Lady: Good heavens, we haven't any slaves today, young lady.

Ngozay's Mother: Hush, child.

Ngozay: But where are the slaves?

Bonnet Lady: Security!

Ngozay: Where are the slaves, ma'am?

Bonnet Lady: Security!

Ngozay's Mother: Hush, child.

Ngozay: I will not hush.

Bonnet Lady: Security!

Ngozay: I will not hush today, Mother.

Ngozay's Mother: Churn the butter, child.

Bonnet Lady: I must ask you to leave the tour now!

Ngozay *(Almost lost in her own thoughts)*: But where are the slaves, ma'am?

Bonnet Lady: Security!

Ngozay's Mother: Hush, child.

Ngozay: But where are the slaves, Ma!?

Bonnet Lady *(Freaking out)*: Security to the fuckin' butter barn—on the double goddammit!!

(The ladies exit, leaving Ngozay alone onstage.)

Ngozay *(Softly)*:
Where
am
I,
in
all
of
this?
Where's my anthem?

(Ngozay speaks over the guitar intro to Psalmayene 24's "Fly.")

Sometimes I wake up and I feel like I'm losing all the black men in D.C.

It all gets jumbled up to me.
From the slave ships,
to the penitentiaries,
to the street corners,
I can't separate it . . .

I don't know,
sometimes I feel like D.C. is a horrible place
for a
black man
to
be . . .

Sorry, Ma . . .

(Psalm appears and sings to Ngozay, our troubled child:)

Psalm *(Sings)*:
Lookin' thru the window of my soul
I see the rain that's gonna wash away my sins
I see the way the lightning that will strike down
my shortcomings,
And I see the road that I am
so scared
to travel
fly . . .
fly . . .
I'm gonna fly to my own heaven . . .

(Psalm continues singing. Ngozay "flies" away as if at play, like a child. Psalm trails off behind her.)

The Ballad of Douglas Martinez

We hear the melancholy strains of an accordion. We see a Chaplinesque actor cross downstage to mime the twelve movements of leaving one land and arriving in another.
Movement:

1—1984.

2—La Union, El Salvador. Life in El Salvador is carefree as war soon erupts. A child dies in the crossfire.

3—The Journey North, leaving El Salvador.

4—The Border. Our hero secures passage as he crosses into Los Estados Unidos (USA).

5—El Norte, America. Our hero is looking for the Lincoln Memorial; he carries a small photo of it.

6—The Journey. He travels across country.

7—The Potomac. Our hero crosses the river in a small boat. He looks a bit like our first President of the United States.

8—Washington, D.C. He finds the Lincoln Memorial—a dream comes true.

9—War, again. Is this a Salvadoran flashback? No, it's—

10—Mount Pleasant, May 5, 1991. The rockets red glare . . .

11—Prince George Country, Ward 9. Our hero finds work. On his way home one night he is confronted and killed.

12—A death figure, the panda, takes him back to El Salvador. Tian Tian, the panda from the start of the play, enters to claim the body of the Salvadoran immigrant. He stands over the body; looks up to the heavens for answers. His movements are slow and ritualistic as he lifts the Salvadoran immigrant with a hand. They hold hands, then in one movement they release hands and softly wave to each other. The Salvadoran immigrant exits. The death figure picks up the photo of the Lincoln Memorial left on the ground and exits.

Lights fade slowly.

We hear a snippet of D.C. radio news.)

D.C. News Anchor Voice-Over: The first reported black on Latino murder occurred tonight in Prince George's County. Ward 9 clergy of every denomination are pleading for calm . . .

(Tian Tian, depressed, walks stage left and lifts himself above the audience. This can be done with a ladder or tree branch.)

National Zoo officials concerned tonight with the erratic behavior of Tian Tian, the panda bear.

Details and your Wizard updates, later, on D.C.'s Quiet Storm, ya'll . . .

(An Anglo woman Zookeeper enters and reaches for the panda's leg. The panda recoils. The Zookeeper removes her gloves and reaches out with her hand. The panda reaches back, there is contact, they touch for a moment. The panda smells the Zookeeper's hand, then slowly moves down and into her arms. The Zookeeper holds the panda as they exit together.)

Salvadoran Jungle Fever/Fiebre de la Selva

Enter a forty-something Salvadoran father, Noe.

Noe: *Kojak, Starsky and Hutch, Happy Days,* este, *Laverne & Shirley.*
Everything I saw on television, was my perception of the
United States when I lived in El Salvador.
   We came to Washington, D.C., in 1984, and landed on
14th and Irving. I said, "Puta! This look more like *Good
Times.*" We didn't know the capital of the United States was
Africa! Puta! Where were the gringos? Where were the tall,
blond, blue-eyed guys from the Peace Corps that I met in
El Salvador?
   I left my country because the Death Squads terrorize us.
I didn't want to come here. I lived in tropical weather. Here
I freeze my huevos in winter!
   I did not go to English class because I thought I would
not need it. Man, was I wrong! We were the new immigrants on the block, it was tough. In high school, blacks
would kick the shit out of us. They would take our lunch
card, books, tokens. There was a lot of violence, people getting stabbed. And so, we started to fight back: "La ley del
machete." We would take machetes to school. Los Negros
started getting hurt, people getting cut. It was nasty. Then
the word got out, "Don't mess with the Salvadorans, the
'migos, 'cause they got the big knives." We had to fight or
die—survival. Finally the black community said, "OK,
these people are here to stay, so we're gonna have to deal
with them."
   There are no black people in El Salvador, so we never
knew any, we never had contact. Salvadorans are very prejudice people. But we have a lot in common. Oh si, we're
both jinchos, country folk, we are both family-oriented, go
to church, we work side by side, we like greasy-ass food, we
like to swear a lot, por la gran puta—we're in the same boat.
   The other day I'm home, and I hear a stranger in my
house . . .

Voice *(From offstage)*: Yo, nigga, where was you man? I was waiting fo' yo ass. I'm at the crib chillin', hit me back, mofo. Word.

(Enrique, a hip-hop b-boy, Salvadoran teenager, enters talking on his cell phone.)

Noe: It was my son Enrique! I told him, *(To Enrique)* "Hey, speak English!"

Enrique: Chill-out, playa.

Noe: Como que "chill-out"? Hablá Inglés, hijo de puta!

Enrique: I'm speaking English, doggy-dog.

Noe *(Pulling The Writer downstage)*: Then, mister Snoop Puffy Doggy brings his girlfriend over for dinner.

(Doorbell rings and a young black girl, Lashanda, enters.)

Lashanda: How you doing, Mr. Ramirez? Oh—como estas?

Noe: Bien, gracias, Lashanda, mucho gusto.

Lashanda *(Crossing to Enrique)*: Enrique, did you holla at Lil' Ray Ray? He be trippin' and shit yo!

Enrique: It's all good, girl.

Lashanda: You gonna be my niggah for life.

(Lashanda exits. Enrique is thrilled, a huge grin on his face, as he looks to his father. He exits. Noe turns to the audience.)

Noe *(Deadpan)*: A la gran puta!

(We hear "The Ghetto" by Too $hort.)

Washington Crosses the Delaware

"The Ghetto" continues as we see General George Washington in his classic pose crossing the Delaware.

The passengers on Washington's life raft are Mohammed, José, the Bonnet Lady, Ngozay and Winston, a D.C. Postal Worker.

The Writer stands across the stage with a lantern, lighting the way for the river crossing.

All: Go George! Go George! Go George! It's your birthday, it's your birthday . . .

(Winston exits the boat. Lights slowly fade.)

Postman Rings Twice

Winston, the Postal Worker, in uniform, speaks with a Jamaican accent to The Writer.

Postal Worker: You darn right I was scared. You darn right I was angry. They're evacuating Capitol Hill and the senate buildings and we're told to go back to work. That everything would be fine.

Everything was not fine.

We were expected to act like military personnel. We are civil servants. There is a big difference.

Pentagon mail workers were told to go back to their work stations that day. Why? Some went back to work like a patriotic duty. Some went back to work because they couldn't afford not to. Some went back to work because we were told . . .

The Writer: . . . that everything would be fine.

Postal Worker: Everything was not fine!

The Writer: I'm agreeing with you, sorry.

Postal Worker: Why were we not given the same information or regard as the rest of the District? Who knew what, when, where? *(The Writer writes quickly)* Look, *(The Writer looks up with full attention)* there is nothing spectacular about Brentwood Post Office. It didn't collapse. Huge clouds did not billow across the District.

But, as you are handling tens of thousands of pieces of mail a day, the contents of just one of these letters . . . *(Removes a white envelope from his postal bag and hands it to The*

Writer) What's in that letter, that little puff of a cloud, was somebody's ground zero.

I have to get back to my route.

(The Postal Worker holds his hand out for the letter. The Writer very slowly and carefully places the letter back into his hand. The Writer wipes his hands on his trousers. He catches himself doing this and feels awkward.)

The Writer *(Slightly embarrassed)*: Thank you for meeting with me, I know how busy you must be.

(The Postal Worker heads out, but stops with one last thought.)

Postal Worker: And when they build all those statues and monuments for the heroes, it would be nice if they remember fallen postal workers, the letter carriers of Washington, D.C.

(He exits. The Writer runs after him.)

The Writer: Sir! Hey, wait!

Mohammed Goes to the MCI Center

We can hear the crowd of the MCI Center. The organ plays "Charge." Mohammed happily walks across the stage in his Redskins jacket and Wizards foam finger. A large Security Guard in a red blazer meets Mohammed at center stage. The Security Guard motions for Mohammed to raise his hands for frisking. Mohammed complies.

The Security Guard whips out a hand wand from his back pocket. Mohammed must turn around. Mohammed must take off his shoes. Mohammed must put his hands behind his head. Mohammed must remove his Redskins jacket. Mohammed must remove his pants.

A White Man crosses, with a shotgun. A Black Man crosses, brandishing a pistol without so much as a wave. A Homeboy in a bandanna crosses with a knife.

Mohammed stands in his boxers. The Security Guard motions him to go. Mohammed gathers his things and walks into the MCI Center.)

MCI Center—Wizard's Cheerleaders

We hear "Who Let the Dogs Out" by Baha Men.

Cheerleaders:
> Woo woo woo woo!
> "Who let the dogs out?"
> Woo woo woo woo!
> Go go Wizards go go!
> Go go Wizards go go!

Cheerleader 1: Awesome! Wheuuuuuuuuuu!
Cheerleader 3: USA!
Cheerleader 1: USA!
Cheerleader 2: USA!
Cheerleaders: Wheuuuuuuuuu!
Cheerleader 1: The terrorists hate America because we're so awesome! Wheuuuu!
Cheerleader 2: Today we have a special birthday celebration, so let's give a cheer!
Cheerleader 1: Ready OK. Give me an M!
Cheerleaders: M!
Cheerleader 1: U!
Cheerleaders: U!
Cheerleader 1: H!
Cheerleaders: H!
Cheerleader 1: A!
Cheerleaders: A!
Cheerleader 1: MMED!
Cheerleaders: MMED!
Cheerleader 1: What's that spell?
Cheerleaders: Uhhhh?
Cheerleader 1: What's that spell??
Cheerleaders: Muhammed!

Cheerleader 1: What's that spell?

Cheerleaders: Go Muhammed!

Cheerleader 1: Awesome!

Mohammed: I spell my name with an "O," not a goddamned "U."

Cheerleaders: Wheuuuuuuuuuuuuu!!

Navy Dress Blues for a Son

Tony Brooks, an African-American man in his funeral Navy blues, enters. He speaks in low and deliberate tones. The Writer listens just offstage.

Tony Brooks: Retired Navy. Thirty years. Worked for an admiral. Put three lovely girls through college. I stay active, try to enjoy my semi-retirement lifestyle.

I used to drive to the Pentagon several times a week for my part-time job.

I have loved ones and business associates on the C, D and E rings.

I have not been back here, to the Pentagon since, well, you know . . . I just didn't want to acknowledge that atrocities of this magnitude could ever happen here at home.

I know a thing or two about tragedy. You see, a few years ago we lost our only son. He was playing high school football, and he died on the gridiron. Heart attack. We never saw it coming, the boy was by all accounts healthy, strapping, in the prime of his youth.

I went crazy. You didn't know you were talking with a crazy man did you?

(Ben Bull enters.)

Ben Bull: Losing a child would make any parent crazy, Tony.

Tony Brooks: But we survived.

Ben Bull: You survived.

Tony Brooks: My wife and I, and we saw through our darkest hour.

(Enter Mrs. Brooks dressed in black, wearing a lovely black funeral hat.)

Mrs. Brooks: I cannot go in there. *(The Brookses embrace)* I will not go in there.

Ben Bull *(Moving toward Mr. and Mrs. Brooks; softly)*: Welcome back to the Pentagon, Tony.

(Mr. Brooks puts on his military hat.

We hear drums. The three slowly walk downstage toward the audience. The couple stops and looks out slightly above the audience, taking in the Pentagon site.

The couple embraces, yet Mr. Brooks never looks away from the site.

Mrs. Brooks—the woman, the mother—quietly weeps. She reaches out for Ben Bull's hand; Ben reaches for hers as well.

We hear Aaron Copland's "Fanfare for the Common Man." The three stand there, in a sort of embrace, a connection, during this "Walkthrough" at the Pentagon.

Mr. Brooks salutes crisply. The three slowly walk offstage. Ben Bull and Mr. Brooks are flanking Mrs. Brooks, who slumps just a bit and cries softly.

The Writer, who has been watching this unfold from offstage, slowly takes the stage holding the Koran. He reads a poem from the book.

Lights shift. There is music/a drone.)

Spokenworld from the District—Anthem

The Writer:
> Dear Ben Bull, I've been thinking about the
> continuity of our text,
> and the conversation we had back at the
> LAX terminal bar
> and this
> anthem you dispatched me to find.
> And it won't be enough sir—
> lullabies and war cries is what
> America wants now.
> Tolstoy could have done it you know
> the petty the grandiose, the monumental the mun-
>   dane.

At this point I just wanna go hide in
Lake Woebegone (or Shady Grove)
and raise children that grow strong,
far away from the Columbines,
holy wars and new Ground Zeros
sure to come,
and new generations of
suicide bombers we'll never stop or truly
understand.
Even though America said,
"Give me liberty or . . ." that other thing . . .
My cab driver gave me a copy of the Koran,
I read here that Mohammed was a prophet—
we are nonprofit . . .
I made some Israeli friends here in
the District, Ben,
I feel terribly guilty though,

(Ben Bull appears for a flash of a moment.)

my mother is half Syrian,
my very own axis of evil for sure—
Arab half-breeds born in occupied Aztlán—
the link is there somewhere.
The link is you, Ben Bull.
I'm invisible here in the land
of the
oblique,
an infiltrator amidst a sea of
waving flags.
I saw the freedom statue above the Capitol,
she looks just like Billie Holiday
facing East,
unable if not unwilling to watch the
onslaught of the Indians to follow,
oh god,
it's September again,
storm clouds on the Hill—
tombstone skies

ghost trains running at full capacity
under the District right now—
I wanna be in that place
between thunder and lighting,
I saw Sitting Bull on the Metro,

(Sitting Bull crosses upstage.)

Apache helicopters over the holy land,
wakes for the living and
wakes for the dead.
Remember, the CIA kills
Che Guevara, now kids wear Che T-shirts
to suburban mosh pits,
Find the Chilean car bombing, Sheridan Circle, 1976,
Pinochet had to have had friends inside the
Beltway to
pull that one off folks.
I went to a five-kegger party with
Chief Rehnquist and the 4th Circuit Judges,
those fuckers can party!
OK, brown is black, they are us,
you are me,
and I am the walrus:
freedom fighters
Iran-Contra
Ollie North
war on drugs
Catholics/Protestants
gay/straight
Tupac/Biggie
Sparta/ *The Handmaid's Tail*
Seven percent of the truth is still the truth, Ben Bull,
the troops are everywhere (says Mick Vranich)
Al Qaeda is in Virginia
black smoke still rising off the Potomac.
We are in our very own history now,
but I'm on a healing timetable as you suggested
Ben,
I find comfort in Larry the parking lot supervisor.

(A Parking Lot Attendant in a red jacket crosses upstage.)

The anarchist anthem is
don't participate
don't participate.
The world's bankers are here this week,
those greedy motherfuckers.

Concentric circles
in Chocolate City,
Córtez and Cuauhtemoc,
Kendra left the District today with
dandelions in her hair.
I am an autumn
Ben Bull
all mixed-up and
connected,
Alice first went through the looking glass
the same year

(Abe Lincoln and Alice cross upstage.)

Lincoln was assassinated . . .
(I'm asking all my writer friends to publish early next
    year).
It's been the summer of
the missing little girl and
June Jordan, rest in peace,
Lionel Hampton, rest in peace
Clarence Henry, Donna Fine and Rebecca Rice
rest in peace,
the list grows daily here.
I have met Pentagon survivors
waiting for me at the stage door, Ben,
and they are weary of our anthems
and remembrance faces

Meth labs in Appalachia
South of the Border here

Mason Dixon Line.
Saddam keeps our minds off Halliburton
Daschle is pissed,
We need rain

well Ben, the Backstreet Boys at Ground Zero
today singing your anthem.
I cannot find it,
I'm sorry Ben Bull from Arlington, Texas,
but I thank you, sir,
for that day at LAX,
you are one of the good guys that's for sure
but I now relieve myself of this mission,
I have failed you badly
I cannot salute the Military Complex.

Because you see, Ben, sometimes the face of terror
comes in forty-one bullets in a vestibule,
sometimes the face of terror wears a
white sheet over its face.
Terror was Jim Crow,
sometimes terror sits in the balcony
sometimes terror kills transgenders in southeast D.C.
(they were only kids)
tonight terror stalks
Montgomery Country and the whole region
(sniper news at eleven)
sometimes the face of terror looks like
Timothy McVeigh,
but right now,
the face of terror
mostly
looks
like
me.

To be or not to be.

(Lights up to reveal U.S. District Judge Leonie M. Brinkema and several Lawyers/Jurists in gray suits and panda masks. The Writer becomes Zacarias Moussaoui at his hearing.)

Judge Brinkema: Mr. Moussaoui I am warning you . . .

Moussaoui: I am a Mujahideen. I am a terrorist in your eyes. As terrorism is like beauty, it is in the eyes of the beholder.

Judge Brinkema: Mr. Moussaoui . . .

Moussaoui: I might be a member of Al Qaeda, Your Honor, but it does not put me on those planes.

Judge Brinkema: I can't accept your guilty plea. Mr. Moussaoui you have an absolute right under our criminal justice system to require the government to put its proof before a jury. I will bar the prosecutors from mentioning at trial that you had tried to plead guilty today.

Moussaoui *(With a slight smile)*: America.

Lawyers/Jurists: Shit.

Judge Brinkema: We are recessed.

Moussaoui: To be or not to be.

Lawyers/Jury: To be or not to be.

Moussaoui: That is the question.

(We hear a low-flying jet. The lights shift. A cell phone rings. The Writer is back to being himself.)

The Writer: Hello? Ben Bull, perfect timing. Listen, the District is turning into my own private Idaho. I'm on trial right now as the twentieth hijacker across the river, and I'm pretty sure I'll be John Walker Lindh in a couple of minutes . . . *(Slaps at a mosquito on his neck)* with West Nile Virus. Look, Pandas are talking to me, trains are derailing, there are donkeys and elephants all over the fucking place and I shot Lincoln in the first act. There are too many guns in this fucking place. Hello? Hello?

(The Writer moves about the stage.)

Can you hear me now? Can you hear me . . .

Look man, I am not a terrorist, I'm an equity actor with a poor dental plan. I know you said my play was a weapon of mass destruction but we have to keep our conversation down low. I don't wanna get tackled to the ground by the Virginia soccer mom in the second row for Christ's sake.

One last thing, Ben, when you said find an *anthem*, did you mean an anthem for the entire nation, an anthem for New York City, an anthem for Flight 93 or an anthem just for the District? That would be helpful with the continuous thing—hello? Ben Bull, goddammit!

(The Writer hangs up the phone. Mohammed enters.)

Mohammed: What did he say, my friend?

(The Writer slumps.)

The Writer: Well I don't know, Mohammed, I don't always get coverage in southwest D.C.
Mohammed: You really fucked up my friend.

What kind of writer are you anyway? *(The Writer shrugs)* I tell you what, come by mosque tomorrow, we pray for second act.

(Mohammed exits.
We hear the panda-masked Jurists/Lawyers:)

Where was the Ethiopian voice?
Where's the Puerto Rican voice, mano?
The nation?
The voice of the voiceless?

The homeless voice?
Where was the professional Hispanic voice?
Where was the transgender voice?
Sauti ya waswahih iko wapi?
Where was the young white male voice, dude?
Where was the voice of the hip-hop generation?

Mr. Wilson *(As a Jurist)*: Our daughter is a lesbian person involved in fringe theater and her voice was missing. C'mon everybody.

(Pandas start to file out. A Panda Baby approaches The Writer.)

Panda Baby *(Signing)*: Where was the deaf voice? *(She exits)*
The Writer: I don't understand you. I don't understand this place at all . . .

(Judge Brinkema is the only one left onstage with The Writer.)

Judge Brinkema: Mister, we don't have all night here. You have the information, you can do this. Back home we say it's in the roux . . .
The Writer: The *rooo*?
Judge Brinkema: The roux, equal parts butter and flour, a thickening agent for sauces that holds the whole dish together. Pay attention to the roux. If you don't find something there listen to the songs of Eva Cassidy, she was a local D.C. girl. Heck, maybe your anthem is in the rattling of the cicadas outside your window.

Just find this thing, find it now.

(Judge Brinkema hums a few lyrics and is gone. We hear the "Strange Fruit" intro.)

Ari Roth: So there we were, at our Peace Cafe, a group of Arabs, and us Jews, on Martin Luther King's birthday at Mimi's American Bistro on 22nd and P.

So, we decide to march to the statue of Gandhi in Dupont Circle. And while marching it occurred to us that we should sing a song. Somebody suggested "We Shall Overcome." Nobody knew the words. A few of us knew the words, but the younger ones didn't.

The anthem for this peace movement has not been written yet.

(Ari Roth exits.)

Cavern Night Club on U Street, Circa 1953

Billie Holiday is escorted to a small stage by an old jazz sidemen. An old-fashioned microphone is put in place by Virgil Smith. Billie sings "Strange Fruit."

> Southern trees bearing strange fruit
> Blood on the leaves
> Blood at the root
> Black bodies swaying in the southern breeze
> Strange fruit hanging from the poplar trees

(We see a vintage film image of the KKK marching on Capitol Hill.)

> Pastoral scenes of the gallant south
> The bulging eyes and the twisted mouth
> The scent of magnolia sweet and fresh
> Then the sudden smell of burning flesh
> Here is a fruit for the crows to pluck
> for the rain to gather
> for the wind to suck
> for the sun to rot
> for the trees to drop

(Billie turns to face The Writer.)

> Here is a strange and bitter crop

(As Billie walks away, we see three elderly, dapper gentlemen standing in front of Ben's Chili Bowl on U street.)

Virgil Smith: I saw Billie Holiday sing "Strange Fruit" at the Cavern back in the day.
Friendly Ray Ford: Say what?
Virgil Smith: 1953.
Friendly Ray Ford: Lady Day?

Virgil Smith: I ain't lying, just ask Friendly Ray Ford and Count Leroy.

Friendly Ray Ford: Jelly Roll Morton was a doorman just down the street.

Virgil Smith: They nearly stabbed poor Jelly Roll to death.

Friendly Ray Ford: I cut a man once.

Moe the Mortician: I was there.

Friendly Ray Ford: Trane, Parker, Duke, Ella—these are the true sounds of Washington, D.C.

Moe the Mortician: Amen, sister.

Virgil Smith: Coleman Hawkins, Lester Young, Les McCann coming out the Blues Alley.

Friendly Ray Ford: That's when Uptown was Uptown!

Virgil Smith: 15th and U Street.

Friendly Ray Ford: Pitts Motor Lodge.

Virgil Smith: The Red Carpet Lounge.

Moe the Mortician: Murphy's Supper Club.

Friendly Ray Ford: Some clubs had the hotel in the back . . .

Virgil Smith: . . . so if it was on . . .

Friendly Ray Ford: . . . go on and get your room on!

(The men all laugh.)

One night, Oscar Brown Junior, jazzman-poet-scholar extraordinaire, said to me, after a Pharaoh Saunders show—

Virgil Smith: Oscar Brown talked to you?

Friendly Ray Ford: Yes, indeed. See, my group, The Sisters of Swing, had opened the show.

Virgil Smith: That's right, I recall. My bad, my bad.

Friendly Ray Ford: Oscar be talkin' about how Plato say that Ethos could ride in on the back on Pathos.

Virgil Smith: Say again?

Friendly Ray Ford: Let me say it one more time for ya now, Ethos, be piggy-backin' on Pathos.

Plato say that music was the best example of this occurrence.

See, Pharoah Saunders could change a room, get us with the pathos of an African drum, then turn us into a mob with the fire coming out his saxophone.

If he had told us to run out on U Street and start a fire
the way Stokely Carmichael did the night Martin was slain,
we woulda done it, sure nuff.
Virgil Smith: Yes, sir.

(Like a boxer, Friendly Ray Ford punctuates each word with a soft left-right jab.)

Friendly Ray Ford: Pathos . . . *(Right jab)* Ethos . . . *(Left jab)*

> Pathos
> loss of life . . .
> Ethos
> a country at war . . .
> Pathos
> sympathy for our neighbors
> bury the dead . . .

(Right jab.)

> Ethos
> spy on our neigbors
> kill all Muslims . . .

(Left jab.)

North.

(Right jab.)

South.

(Left jab.)

Moe the Mortician: Pathos . . .

Friendly Ray Ford:
> Blood of Christ.

(Right jab.)

Virgil Smith: Ethos . . .

Friendly Ray Ford:
> Greed is good
> Enron . . .

(Right-left combo.)

All: Pathos/Ethos.

Virgil Smith: Now do Catholic priests fall in the Ethos or the Pathos?

Friendly Ray Ford:
> Either
> Or.

> The point is, my man Plato knew that music was dangerous three thousand years before Miles.
> Dig this: if you ever find yourself at the Metro station (Waterfront, Southwest), and you waitin' for the Greenline heading to Anacostia . . .

Virgil Smith: You mean the Greenline Branch Avenue?

Friendly Ray Ford: I mean the Greenline heading to Anacostia! When that train pulls into the station, see the wheels and the brakes be grinding in perfect pitch with Miles Davis's trumpet.

Moe the Mortician: Say what?

Friendly Ray Ford: Listen to the record *Big Fun!*

Virgil Smith: Now you talkin' like a crazy old fool.

Friendly Ray Ford: No, sir, it's the truth. Scout's honor.

Virgil Smith: I saw Miles in '63 just down the road here and I say you talkin' crazy.

Friendly Ray Ford: Look here, let's us stroll down there right now and I will prove my scientifical theory to ya'll. C'mon.

(The men move a few steps downstage. The lights shift and we are at the Metro station standing near a strip of Metro lights. The Writer is waiting for a train to take him to Union Station and the airport. He listens to the jazz men. We hear the Greenline train pulling into the station. The Metro lights flicker.)

Here come the train ya'll . . .

(The sound of the train, the brakes and the squeals of the wheels take our attention.)

Metro Conductor Voice-Over: . . . Waterfront Station, Southwest, doors open on the left, this is your Anacostia . . .

(Friendly Ray Ford turns on his tape player.)

Friendly Ray Ford: Here come Miles. Laying it down solid . . .

(We hear Miles Davis's Big Fun *sweetly creeping in. We hear the train. The sounds merge and, yes, there is a similar pitch.)*

Ya'll hear that? I told you so, I told you so!
Virgil Smith: Ah shucks.
Moe the Mortician: Miles and the train to Anacostia!
Friendly Ray Ford: Beautiful man.

(The jazz men exit shaking their heads, except for Friendly Ray Ford. The music of Miles Davis continues to play under the following:)

The trains in D.C. are still rollin'. Life keeps rollin'.
The Writer: Rolling . . .
Friendly Ray Ford: Continuous.
The Writer: Continuous . . .

(The Writer hands Friendly Ray Ford the piece of collard green from before.)

Friendly Ray Ford: Right un'neath your feet the whole time, my man.

(Friendly Ray Ford begins to exit.)

The Writer: Gracias.

(Friendly Ray Ford turns cooly, the way only a jazz veteran can.)

Friendly Ray Ford: De nada.

(He is gone.
*   We feel the rush of the train and see the flicker of the lights. The*
Writer records the train. People cross the stage as the Metro comes
and goes. The Writer crosses upstage to the airport.)

Airport Announcer: Welcome to Dulles International Airport. Due
to heightened security, please . . .

(Tian Tian, carrying a suitcase, crosses the stage. The Writer
stands at a security checkpoint. Miles continues. The lights slowly
fade to Africa-America. Blackout.)

The End

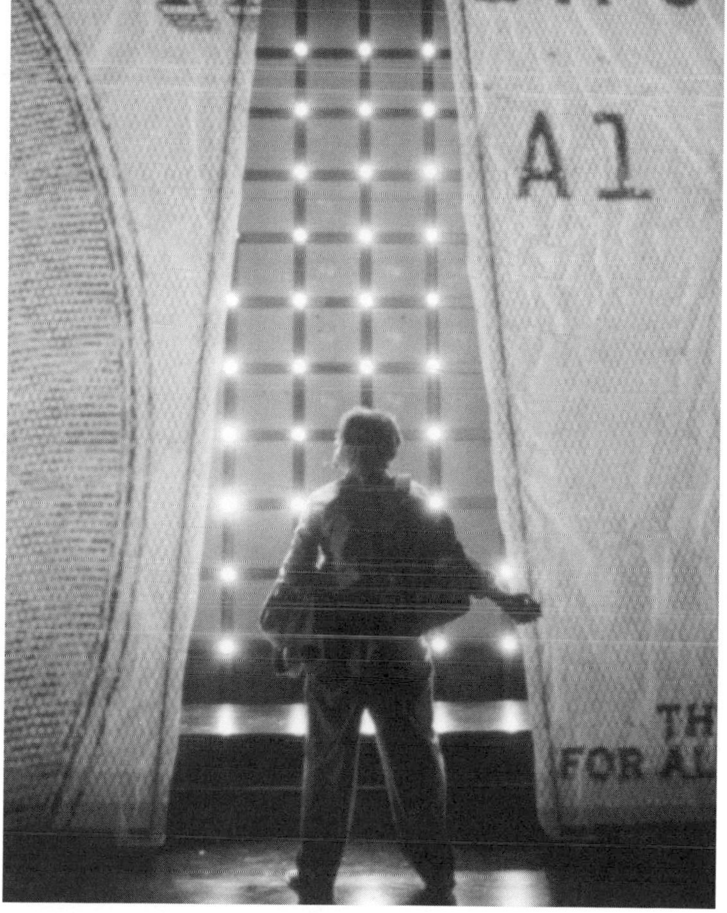
BAO
A1

Afterword

A REPORT FROM ANOTHER SUBURBAN GROUND ZERO:
BEING A PLAYWRIGHT UNDER SNIPER FIRE;
OR WHAT HAPPENED TO THE WHITE MAN IN THE WHITE VAN?

By Richard Montoya

We closed *Anthems* two days ago but I continue to linger here in
the District of Columbia. I told myself I was staying to say so
long to some of the older, more frail folks whose lives we bor-
rowed for the stage; a tinge of sadness as I do not know if I will
see these wonderful people (or place) again. I needed a kind of
closure after so much time invested here—I feel like the last
man standing—I've seen seasons change here many times. But I
linger too because once again D.C. is such a strange and dangerous place to be at this moment.

From my Arena Stage–provided ninth-floor apartment I can
see the ominous Pentagon directly in front of my laptop, just
across the Potomac River there. I realize now that I am sitting
just this side of a huge sliding window, a perfect brown target
for the mad, racially democratic sniper down below.

My thoughts are very much on the notion of terror. This
terror mainly seems to hover over the suburbs of Maryland and
Virginia, which somehow makes it more horrifying and sensa-
tional to the media. I checked the police blotter just now and
there were as many murders in the District this weekend as the
entire bloody rampages in the burbs of this region. Even as

Dubya tries in vain to keep our minds on Saddam, every news channel is providing All Sniper All the Time coverage. Terror is not created equal.

The madness is continuous, and the mundane becomes murderous, and in the midst of these crazy times is *Anthems*. It just keeps reverberating inside my bones.

Anthems is a hip-hop play without trying to be. We sampled, mixed and remixed living histories. *Anthems* was my mind. *Anthems* was in touch with its Negritude. Some said it was a play for black folks—so be it. What *Anthems* became was a bloody valentine in the short period of time we performed it. We kept up with and, in some cases, out-paced the newspaper headlines. (Months before Chandra Levy was found in Rock Creek Park, I had written that she was found in the exact spot where her decomposed body was found, a Salvadoran man the chief suspect.)

This may be one of the first instances where subscriber audiences risked their lives to come to the theater; they traveled from the suburbs to well-lit parking lots, filled up their gas tanks for the ride home on the Beltway and, for the most part, filled up the theater throughout this suburban jihad.

Anthems would never have been possible without Arena Stage, Molly Smith and an incredible ensemble led by Joseph Kamal and Johanna Day. Joseph, fresh from the New York City production of *Homebody/Kabul*, lent so much humanity (and some text) to the creation of Mohammed, the cab driver. Miss Day originated roles in *How I Learned to Drive* and *Proof*, for which she won a Tony nomination. She chose to do *Anthems* because it was a new play, and that emboldened me to no end. It is a true testament to our director, Charles Randolph-Wright, who cast these folks, as well as the amazing Jay Patterson who also lent text, the marvelous Shona Tucker and Gentleman Bill Grimmette.

Culture Clash brought in Howard University's own bright light, Nikki Jean, and my brother, Psalmayene 24, who wrote the song "Fly," the story of go-go music and created the character Cisero Jones.

I thank all the folks we interviewed, especially Kendra Ware; Ngozay T. Robinson; Jaylee Mead; Bill Fleishell; Denise Schneider; Oscar Brown, Junior; Sweet Honey in the Rock; Mr.

Carlisle Sealy; Michael Slate; The Artists Network; Sol y Soul; Friendly Ray Ford and writer Richard Talavera for his poem "I'm in Heaven." Gracias Anne "It's in the roux" Kennedy, Alex Nichols and Timothy M. Thompson. And finally thanks to my rock, Ric Salinas.

Anthems should never have an asterisk next to it because all of the Culture Clash guys did not perform it—that will matter little in the final analysis or when new generations tackle the work. What will matter is that it was a huge leap for Culture Clash: a mature play that provided work for so many gifted actors, designers and a director we were lucky to get. Blackout!

> From 9/11 to a sniper named Muhammed with a U!
> What a year.
> Jesus. Blood in blood out,
> the mundane became the monumental.

October 2002

Founded in 1984 on Cinco de Mayo in San Francisco's Mission District, **CULTURE CLASH** is Richard Montoya, Ric Salinas and Herbert Siguenza. For the past several years, Culture Clash has been focusing on site-specific theater, weaving personal narratives culled from interviews into an ongoing dramatic tapestry. Theater companies in Miami, San Diego, New York and San Francisco, among others, have commissioned Culture Clash to create performance pieces specifically for their cities. The fact that they were working on a performance piece about the Nation's Capital (*Anthems: Culture Clash in the District*) at the time of the terrorist attacks places them on the frontlines of cultural and artistic response to crisis. Their work gives immediate dramatic voice and expression to people in a certain time and place. It is theater of the moment, written and performed first for the people and communities on which it is based, and secondarily for a broader audience. Culture Clash uses "performance collage" to bring history, geography, "urban excavation," "forensic poetry" and storytelling together in a contemporary, movable theater narrative through a Chicano point of view— what Guillermo Gómez-Peña describes as "reverse anthropology."

Culture Clash's theatrical work includes *The Mission* (1988), which ran at the Los Angeles Theater Center in 1990, followed by the hit *A Bowl of Beings* (1991). In 1992, *A Bowl of Beings* received its television premiere on the PBS series *Great Performances*. *S.O.S.—Comedy for These Urgent Times* (1992) examined the Los Angeles uprising and the Rodney King beating, and played at the Japan American Theatre in the Little Tokyo area of Los Angeles and Magic Theatre, Inc. in San Francisco. *Carpa Clash* (1993), a tribute to the great UFW President César Chávez, played at the Mark Taper Forum in Los Angeles. *Radio*

Mambo: Culture Clash Invades Miami (1995) premiered in Miami and toured nationally.

In 1998, Culture Clash unveiled two world premieres: *Bordertown* for San Diego Repertory Theatre and *The Birds*, a musical adaptation of Aristophanes' classic for South Coast Repertory and Berkeley Repertory Theatre. *Nuyorican Stories* (1999) was performed at INTAR in New York's Off-Broadway row. *Anthology* (2000), a fifteen-year retrospective, had extended runs in L.A., San Francisco and San Diego. *Mission Magic Mystery Tour* (2000) played at San Francisco's Eureka Theatre Company. *Anthems: Culture Clash in the District* (2002) premiered at Arena Stage in Washington, D.C. Their latest work, *Chavez Ravine* will have its world premiere in spring 2003 at the Mark Taper Forum in Los Angeles.

Additionally, in 1992, Culture Clash co-produced, wrote and starred in an award-winning short film, *Columbus on Trial,* directed by Lourdes Portillo. In 1993, Culture Clash made television history with the first-ever Chicano sketch TV show: *Culture Clash,* which aired on several FOX markets. In 2002, Culture Clash produced interactive video installations for Cheech Marin's *Chicano Now: American Expressions* national touring art show.

Culture Clash is the recipient of numerous awards and grants, including a grant from the Rockefeller Foundation, the Latino Spirit Award, the Los Angeles Hispanic Media Award, the Nosotros Golden Eagle Award for Outstanding Theater Group and others. Their videos, short fillms and art exhibits have been shown at The Smithsonian; the Whitney Museum of American Art; Sundance Film Festival; the San Juan, Puerto Rico Film and Video Festival; the Art Institue of Boston and Galería de la Raza.